# The New Paper Style

# The New Paper Style

## Mimi Christensen

**Sterling Publishing Co., Inc. New York**
A Sterling/Chapelle Book

# Chapelle Ltd.

Owner: Jo Packham

Editor: Leslie Ridenour
Art Director: Linda Orton

Staff: Ann Bear, Areta Bingham, Kass Burchett, Marilyn Goff, Holly Hollingsworth, Susan Jorgensen, Barbara Milburn, Karmen Quinney, Cindy Stoeckl, Gina Swapp, Sara Toliver

Project Photography: Kevin Dilley for Hazen Photography

## Special Thanks

Several projects in this book were created with outstanding and innovative products provided by the following manufacturers and retailers: DecoArt/Americana®, Delta Paints, EK Success, Fiskars, Hollywood Trim/Prym Dritz, Walnut Hollow

**Library of Congress Cataloging-in-Publication Data**

Christensen, Mimi.
   The new paper style / Mimi Christensen.
     p. cm.
   "A Sterling/Chapelle book."
   Includes index.
   ISBN 0-8069-3651-7
   1. Paper work.  I. Title

   TT870.C497 2000
   745.54--dc21

00-061894

10 9 8 7 6 5 4 3 2

**A Sterling/Chapelle Book**

Published by Sterling Publishing Company, Inc.
387 Park Avenue South, New York, NY 10016
© 2001 by Mimi Christensen
Distributed in Canada by Sterling Publishing
% Canadian Manda Group, One Atlantic Avenue, Suite 105
Toronto, Ontario, Canada M6K 3E7
Distributed in Great Britain and Europe by Cassell PLC
Wellington House, 125 Strand, London WC2R 0BB, England
Distributed in Australia by Capricorn Link (Australia) Pty Ltd.
P.O. Box 704, Windsor, NSW 2756 Australia
Printed in China
All Rights Reserved

Sterling ISBN 0-8069-3651-7

If you have any questions or comments, please contact:

Chapelle Ltd., Inc.
P.O. Box 9252
Ogden, UT 84409
Phone: (801) 621-2777
FAX: (801) 621-2788
e-mail: chapelle@chapelleltd.com
web site: www.chapelleltd.com

To contact Sarah Lugg, log on to her web site at www.sarahlugg.com

All photographs on pages 96–103 Copyright © 1999 Sarah Lugg.

# About the Author

Mimi Christensen remembers growing up on a ranch in Southern Colorado being extremely happy and content. Her parents had a positive influence on her, including their encouragement and interest in her artistic endeavors. Her father, in addition to running the ranch, was a carpenter; so there was never a shortage of tools, scraps of wood, nails, and imagination. Her mother was an artist, seamstress, excellent storyteller, and nurturer. Money was the only shortage they experienced, but lack of money helped Mimi and all of her siblings develop in a creative way.

For the past 18 years, Mimi has been a free-lance designer. She works with fabric, stuffing, batting, embroidery floss, ribbons, beads, paints, wood, paper, and just about anything else, which might be transformed into something beautiful.

Mimi has designed projects for Cranston Print Work's web site, V.I.P. Fabrics, Concord House Fabrics, Benartex Fabrics, and C.M. Offray & Son Ribbons. Her work has been featured several times in ads, and she has designed television projects for Fairchild Processing Inc. In addition, she has taught doll-making, coproduced a television special for public television, lectured, coordinated cloth-doll exhibits, and has been featured in many magazines, including Good Housekeeping, Woman's Day, Soft Dolls and Toys, and others.

# Acknowledgments

This book is dedicated to Jo Packham, whose friendship and wisdom have inspired me to achieve goals I never thought possible.

# Table of Contents

# Introduction

Paper was part of my own creative childhood experience. My mother allowed my brothers and sisters and me cut out pictures from the large Montgomery Ward catalogue. We pasted these pictures onto the inside 'walls' of old shoe boxes. We would then cut a rectangular 'window' in the lid and tape colored cellophane over the opening. A peep hole cut into one end of the shoe box let us look into our little 'room.' The colored cellophane changed the light into a red or yellow hue and we could see all the pictures in amber or rosy hues.

Today, I find myself in a world with an almost endless supply of paper—from lined paper used for homework to printed paper used in magazines, books, and newspapers; from scrapbook pages, tissue paper, gift wrappings, and wallpaper to bank checks, grocery bags, and cardboard boxes.

This book shows you how to transform ordinary paper into objects for decorating your home, for embellishing gifts, and for entertaining. Discover ways to use paper objects to grace a table, decorate for holidays, create frames for special photographs, accent a special room, or keep your children busy on a rainy day. Get your scissors, glue, and imagination, and have fun!

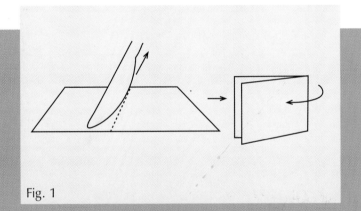

Fig. 1

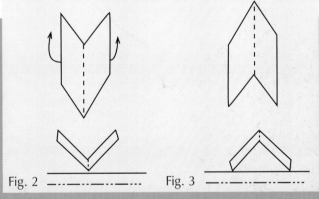

Fig. 2    Fig. 3

## Paper Basics

Many of the projects in this book require the use of scoring and folding—basic paper manipulation techniques. These easy to master methods will make crafting with paper practically painless.

## Scoring

Refer to Fig. 1. Using a ruler and pencil, measure and mark areas to be folded. Using a bone folder or butter knife, score paper along the pencil line. Fold along score.

## Folding

*Valley Fold:*
Refer to Fig. 2. A valley fold means the paper is folded so the fold line becomes the bottom of a valley and the edges of the paper are pointing upward when resting on the work surface.

*Mountain Fold:*
Refer to Fig. 3. A mountain fold means the paper is folded so the fold line is like the peak of a mountain with the edges of the paper pointing downward when resting on the work surface.

# Party Hats

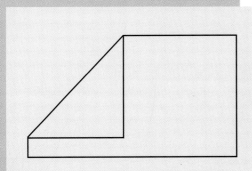

Fig. 1

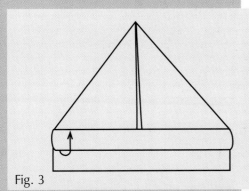

Fig. 2

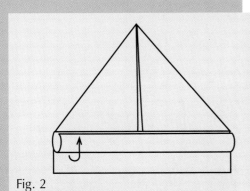

Fig. 3

*Supplies:*
• Double-sided tape
• Lace medallions: black (2)
• Newspaper: 18" x 24"
• White fabric glue

*Instructions for Sailor Hat:*
1. Fold paper in half to 12" x 18". Place on work surface.

2. Refer to Fig. 1. Fold each corner of folded edge down at right angles to center approximately 2" from bottom edges.

3. Refer to Fig. 2. Fold length of upper bottom edge in half, so raw edge meets raw edges of folded-over corners.

4. Refer to Fig. 3. Fold edge up again where raw edges meet, covering folded over corners.

5. Turn hat over on work surface. Repeat Steps 3–4 for remaining bottom edge.

6. Attach double-sided tape inside folded up edges. Press newspaper onto tape to secure.

7. Glue lace medallion onto side of hat.

9

*Instructions for Robin Hood Hat:*

1. Repeat Steps 1–5 for Instructions for Sailor Hat on page 9.

2. Refer to Fig. 4. Turn hat so one pointed side is facing forward. Overlap folded bottom edges. Attach double-sided tape under overlap. Remove protective covering from tape and press overlap onto tape to secure.

3. Refer to Fig. 5. Fold one pointed edge back toward top of hat. Attach double-sided tape under overlap. Press overlap onto tape to secure.

4. Glue lace medallion onto side of hat.

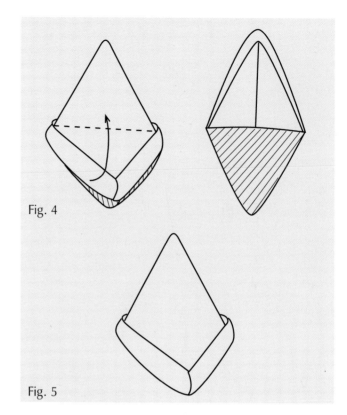

Fig. 4

Fig. 5

## Masquerade Ball

Watch your guests' eyes light up as they unravel a party ball designed especially for them. Using colorful streamers of crepe paper, start wrapping into a ball shape, much in the same manner as rolling a ball of yarn. As you go, add tiny treasures along the way. The festive surprises can include money, charms, confetti shapes, candy, jewelry, and fortunes. Tie your ball with a beautiful ribbon and attach a charm or name tag.

# Pinwheels

*Supplies:*
- Acrylic paints
- Colored paper: 8½" x 11"
- Paintbrush: flat
- Paper scissors
- Pencil
- Push pin
- Ruler
- Wooden dowel: ⁷⁄₁₆"-diameter x 12"–22"

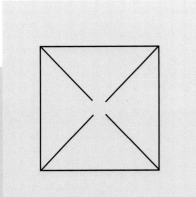

Fig. 1

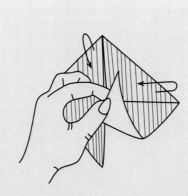

Fig. 2

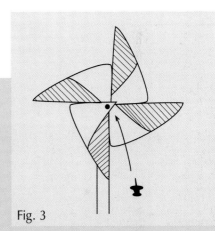

Fig. 3

*Instructions:*

1. Paint dowel with paint to coordinate with paper. Paint head of push pin to match or contrast. Allow to dry.

2. Using ruler and pencil, draw a 7" square.

3. Refer to Fig. 1. Cut a 4¼" slit, from each corner toward center of square.

4. Refer to Fig. 2. Fold left corner of each resulting triangle shape toward center of square.

5. Refer to Fig. 3. Insert push pin through all four corners and through square center. Push firmly into painted dowel.

## Old Letters & Silverware Shadow Box

The sad thing about precious memorabilia is that it is usually tucked away in some drawer where it cannot be enjoyed. Why not make a photocopied collage of treasured letters and envelopes and use it as a backdrop for your grandmother's old silverware or dad's antique pocket watch? Mounted in a shadow box, they will present a nostalgic reminder of days gone by.

## Elegant Bill Portfolios

Important presentations call for that extra touch of class. For a simple, but polished look, roll your document within a piece of corrugated paper and tie with cording. Or, tear the top edge of a piece of handmade paper, fold into thirds with your papers inside, and bind it together with silk ribbon. For interesting ornamentation that will create a lasting impression, enhance purchased portfolios with old purse clasps or metal scraps.

# Little Folded Book

*Supplies:*
- Colored cardboard: 3¾" x 7½"
- Colored printed papers: contrasting, 12" square (3)
- Double-sided tape
- Fabric scissors
- Paper glue
- Paper scissors
- Paper scraps
- Pencil
- Ruler
- Silk ribbon: green, 7mm (24")

*Instructions:*
1. Cut two 3" strips from each printed paper.

2. Refer to Folding on page 7 and Fig. 1. Accordion-fold one strip at 3" intervals, making a valley fold first. Note: The area within a mountain and valley fold is a page.

3. Refer to Fig. 2. Attach double-sided tape onto left edge of last page that begins at a valley fold.

4. Refer to Fig. 3. Trim paper to right of tape.

5. Refer to Fig. 4. Attach remaining strip of same paper onto tape, butting left edge of second strip to last fold of first strip.

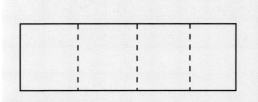

Fig. 1

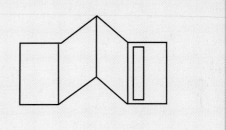

Fig. 2

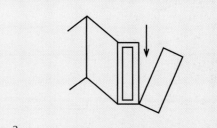

Fig. 3

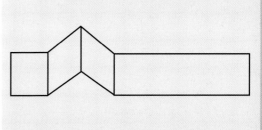

Fig. 4

6. Refer to Fig. 5. Continue folding strip as in Step 2 on page 17.

7. Cut off remaining paper at last mountain fold so all pages are even.

8. Refer to Fig. 6. Fold one strip of second paper ½" from short edge with a mountain fold.

9. Beginning at fold, repeat Steps 2–6.

10. Cut off remaining paper at last valley fold so all pages are even.

11. Refer to Fig. 7. Attach double-sided tape onto ½" at beginning of paper.

12. Refer to Fig 8. Attach onto wrong side top edge of first folded paper—continuing in a vertical direction from first folded paper.

13. Fold one strip of third paper ½" from short edge with a valley fold.

14. Beginning at fold, repeat Steps 2–7 making a mountain fold first.

15. Repeat Step 11.

16. Refer to Fig 9. Attach onto wrong side right edge of second folded paper—continuing in a horizontal direction from second folded paper.

17. Cut two 3¾" squares from cardboard.

18. Glue center of ribbon onto one cardboard square. Note: This will be the back cover.

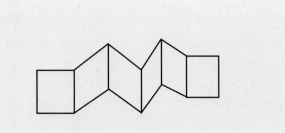

Fig. 5

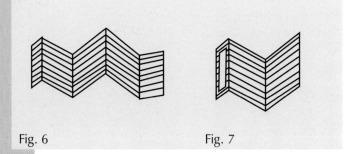

Fig. 6     Fig. 7

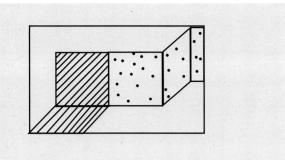

Fig. 8

Fig. 9

19. Cut two 3" squares from one printed paper.

20. Refer to Fig. 10. Center and glue one paper square onto each cardboard square, covering ribbon. Allow to dry.

21. Refer to Fig. 11. Center and glue first page of first folded paper onto wrong side of front cover, and last page of third folded paper onto wrong side of back cover, making certain ribbon is horizontal. Allow to dry.

22. Wrap ribbon ends around to front. Tie ribbon in a bow. Using fabric scissors, trim ribbon ends at a 45° angle.

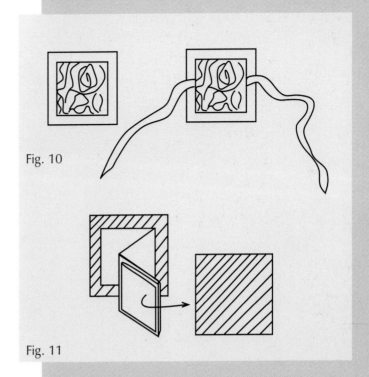

Fig. 10

Fig. 11

# Box of Note Cards & Envelopes

*Supplies:*
- Bone folder or butter knife
- Colored papers for note cards and envelopes: contrasting, 8½" x 11" (6)
- Colored printed card stock for box: 12" x 13"
- Decorative-edged scissors: mini scallop; ripple
- Double-sided tape with protective covering
- Embellishments: cupid charms (2); key charms (2); large heart bead
- Fabric scissors
- Metallic thread
- Needle
- Paper glue
- Paper scissors
- Pencil
- Ruler
- Silk ribbon: lavender, 4mm (18")
- Suede paper scraps

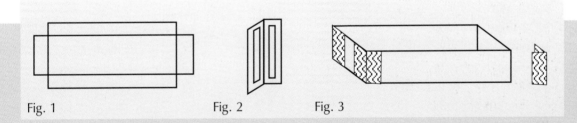

Fig. 1          Fig. 2          Fig. 3

*Instructions for Box:*

1. Using paper scissors, cut a 6" x 13" rectangle from printed card stock. Place printed side of card stock down on work surface. Measure and mark 1½" around all sides.

2. Refer to Fig. 1. Cut away all corners.

3. Using bone folder or butter knife, score fold lines. Fold four sides upward.

4. Using paper scissors, cut four 1" x 1½" corner pieces from suede paper scraps. Using ripple decorative-edged scissors, trim 1½" edges.

5. Refer to Fig. 2. Fold corner pieces in half lengthwise with suede on outside. Attach double-sided tape onto each side of fold on inside.

6. Refer to Fig. 3. Remove protective covering from tape. Attach corner pieces onto each outside corner of box.

7. For box lid, repeat Steps 1–3, cutting a 4⅛" x 11⅛" rectangle.

8. Repeat Steps 4–6, cutting four ½" x 1" corner pieces.

*Instructions for Envelope:*

1. Using paper scissors, cut an 8" x 11" rectangle from colored paper.

2. Refer to Fig. 4. Draw a line ¼" in from left and bottom edges. Draw a line ⅞" in from top edge.

3. Refer to Fig. 5. Draw a line 4⅛" in from left edge.

4. Refer to Fig. 6. Cut away all corners.

5. Refer to Fig. 7. Trim corners of top edge at a slight angle.

6. Using bone folder or butter knife, crease fold lines.

7. Fold left and bottom edges inward.

8. Refer to Fig. 8. Apply glue to top of folded edges. Fold right edge over onto glue. Press and allow to dry.

9. Attach double-sided tape along top edge. Note: Leave the protective covering on tape until ready to seal the envelope.

*Instructions for The Key to My Heart Note Card:*
1. Using paper scissors, cut a 5¼" x 9½" rectangle from colored paper.

2. Refer to Fig. 9. Using mini scallop decorative-edged scissors, trim right edge of paper.

3. Fold paper in half lengthwise so border shows about ⅛".

4. Stitch key charms onto paper with metallic thread. Stitch a curved line (about 1½" long) to

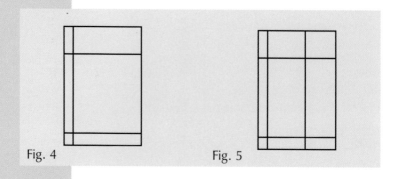

Fig. 4    Fig. 5

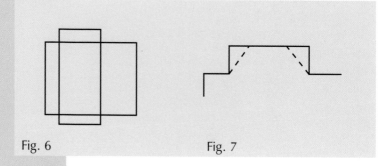

Fig. 6    Fig. 7

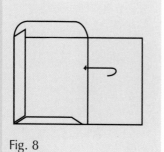

Fig. 8

center of paper and attach heart bead.

*Instructions for Silk Ribbon-edged Note Card and Cupid-On-A-String Note Card:*
1. Using paper scissors, cut two 7½" x 9½" rectangles from colored papers. Accordion-fold in thirds.

2. Whipstitch around edges of one note card with silk ribbon. Note: Make certain to catch the tail of the ribbon in the stitches.

3. Using mini scallop decorative-edged scissors, cut two corners from front of remaining note card.

4. Stitch one cupid charm onto right side of note card with metallic thread. Stitch a line to left side of note card and attach remaining cupid charm.

# Folded Box

## Supplies:
- Bone folder or butter knife
- Colored card stock: 8½" x 11"
- Paper glue
- Paper scissors
- Pencil
- Sealing wax with stamp and matches

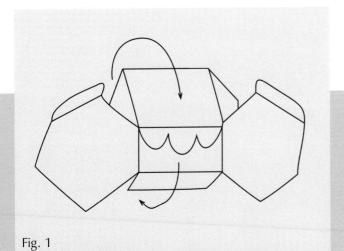

Fig. 1

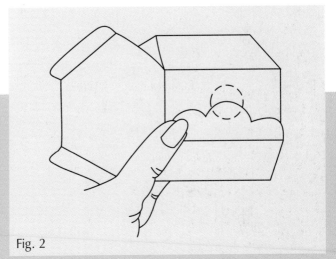

Fig. 2

## Instructions:

1. Photocopy Folded Box Template on page 24. Cut out copied template.

2. Using template, trace and cut box from card stock.

3. Using bone folder or butter knife, score fold lines. Fold sections upward, folding A, B, C, D, and E tabs at a 90° angle.

4. Refer to Fig. 1. Roll box so it is slightly circular in shape, leaving scalloped flap outside box. Glue flap to outside of box.

5. Insert tab D into box between tabs C and B. Insert tab E into box between tabs B and A.

6. Refer to Fig. 2. Following manufacturer's instructions, seal box flap with sealing wax.

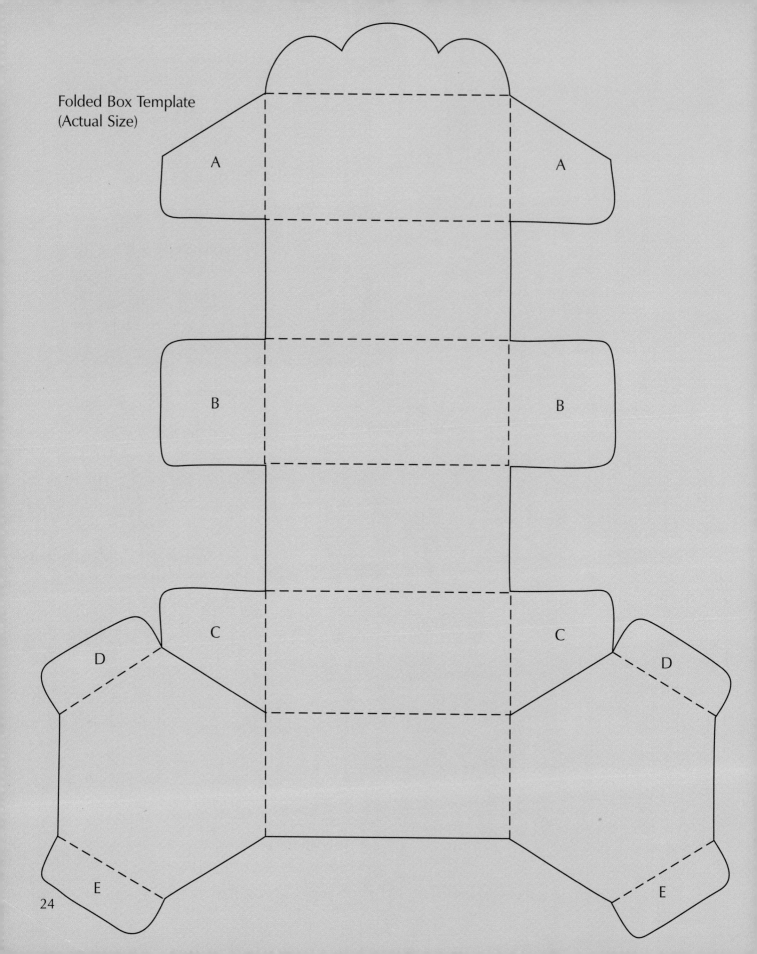

Folded Box Template
(Actual Size)

A

A

B

B

C

C

D

D

E

E

24

## Oriental Tube Invitations

Make your guests feel very special by inviting them in style. These decorated scroll holders were made from cardboard mailing tubes. They were wrapped in handmade papers and adorned with ribbons and charms for an Oriental touch. Decorate the tubes to introduce your party theme and the only worry you will have is making the party as noteworthy as the invitations!

25

Art for the Home

## Framed Envelopes

This subtle yet sophistocated piece of functional artwork was created by photocopying and tracing the Framed Envelope Template on page 28 onto several subtle shades of colored card stock. The envelopes were folded as indicated on the template and secured with antique buttons and embroidery floss. Professionally framed for display, the envelopes can be used to hold cherished momentos, like baby's first curl.

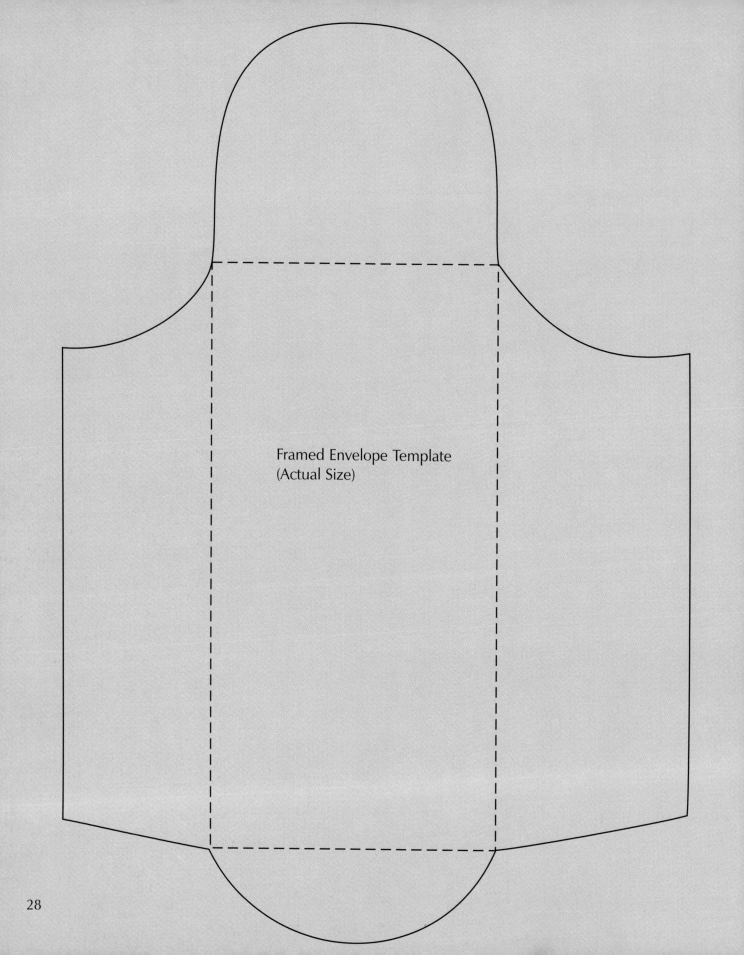

Framed Envelope Template
(Actual Size)

28

Candle Cuffs & Napkin Rings

*Supplies:*
- Bone folder or butter knife
- Card stock: off-white, 8½" x 11" (3)
- Craft knife or rotary cutter
- Decorative-edged scissors: scallop
- Paper glue
- Paper punch: fleur de lis
- Pencil
- Scissors
- Tape measure

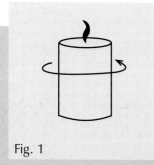

Fig. 1

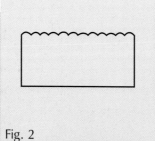

Fig. 2

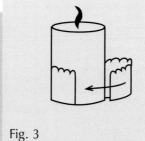

Fig. 3

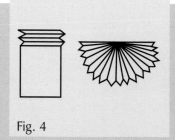

Fig. 4

*Instructions for Round Candle Cuff:*

1. Refer to Fig. 1. Measure circumference of candle plus ½" for Measurement A. Measure height of candle. Divide height by three for Measurement B.

2. Cut a rectangle to Measurement A x Measurement B from one piece of card stock.

3. Refer to Fig. 2. Using decorative-edged scissors, trim one edge, creating the cuff.

4. Refer to Fig. 3. Wrap cuff around base of candle. Overlap short edges and glue in place. Note: If the candle is square, score the corners with a bone folder or butter knife and fold them so they fit the candle as closely as possible.

5. Refer to Fig. 4. Cut a 3" square from card stock. Accordion-fold square with ¼" folds and fold in half to create a fan shape. Glue folds together at center and where ends meet to hold fan in place.

6. Refer to Fig. 5. Cut a ¼" strip from card stock. Roll ends of strip to create S-shaped scrolls.

7. Refer to Fig. 6. Glue scroll onto fan with one end on base of fan and remaining end under right edge of fan.

8. Repeat Steps 5–7 for enough fans and scrolls to evenly circle candle.

9. Refer to Fig. 7. Glue fans and scrolls onto candle cuff.

*Instructions for Napkin Ring:*
1. Cut a 2¼" x 5½" rectangle from one piece of card stock.

2. Refer to Fig. 8. Punch along one long edge of rectangle. Repeat for remaining long edge.

3. Using decorative-edged scissors, trim punched edges. Note: Take care to avoid cutting into the punched border.

4. Overlap short edges and glue in place, creating napkin ring.

5. Repeat Steps 5–7 for Instructions for Round Candle Cuff to create fan and scroll for napkin ring.

6. Center and glue fan and scroll onto front of napkin ring.

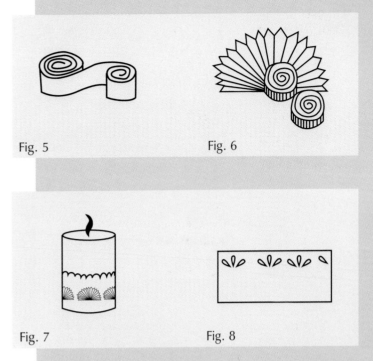

Fig. 5    Fig. 6

Fig. 7    Fig. 8

*Instructions for Pleated Candle Cuff:*
1. Measure circumference of candle. Double measurement for Measurement A. Measure height of candle. Divide height by three for Measurement B.

2. Cut a rectangle to Measurement A x Measurement B from one piece of card stock.

3. Pleat length of rectangle with ¼" pleats.

4. Stretch pleats around candle, creating cuff. Overlap short edges and glue in place.

5. Cut a ½" strip to circumference of candle plus 2" from card stock. Wrap strip around pleated cuff. Overlap short edges and glue in place.

6. Cut a ½" strip from card stock. Roll ends of strip to create S-shaped scroll.

7. Glue scroll onto center of strip on candle cuff.

# Accent Blocks

*Supplies for Basic Block:*
- Bone folder or butter knife
- Card stock or lightweight corrugated card board: 8½" x 11" (3)
- Craft scissors and/or craft knife
- Paper glue
- Pencil
- Ruler

*Instructions for Basic Block:*
1. Photocopy Basic Block Templates on pages 36–37. Cut out copied templates.

2. Using template, trace and cut box pieces from card stock or lightweight corrugated cardboard.

3. Using bone folder or butter knife, score fold lines.

4. Glue A onto a and E onto e.

5. Refer to Folding on page 7. Fold block together, making valley folds, and glue tabs inside block.

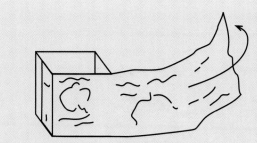

Fig. 1

*Additional Supplies for Oriental Block:*
- Printed paper with oriental characters: 8½" x 11" (4)
- Stickers

*Additional Instructions for Oriental Block:*
1. Following Instructions for Basic Block, make block from lightweight corrugated cardboard.

2. Cut width of printed paper to fit sides of block.

3. One side at a time, apply paper glue onto block. Refer to Fig. 1. Glue paper onto block, smoothing any wrinkles. Overlap paper pieces as desired, taking care not to cover main design. Allow to dry.

4. Apply stickers onto sides and top of box as desired.

*Additional Supplies for Button Block:*
- Colored paper: 8½" x 11"
- Colored printed papers: 8½" x 11" (2)
- Decorative buttons
- Decorative-edged scissors: ripple
- Fine-tipped marking pen: black
- Hot-glue gun and glue sticks
- Metallic paper: scraps
- Needle and embroidery floss to match project
- Paper scissors

*Additional Instructions for Button Block:*
1. Following Instructions for Basic Block on page 33, make block from lightweight corrugated cardboard.

2. Using paper scissors, cut four 2" strips of paper for vertical corners of box.

3. Refer to Fig. 2. Fold strips in half, lengthwise. Glue folded strips onto box corners.

4. Refer to Fig. 3. Repeat Steps 2–3 for top and bottom edges of box.

5. Using decorative-edged scissors, cut a 3½" square from contrasting solid paper.

6. Refer to Fig. 4. Adhere square diagonally onto one side of box with paper glue.

7. Photocopy Letter Template. Cut out copied template.

8. Using template, pencil, and paper scissors, trace and carefully cut letter from metallic paper.

9. Using needle and embroidery floss, stitch two buttons onto letter. Adhere letter onto side of box opposite colored square with paper glue.

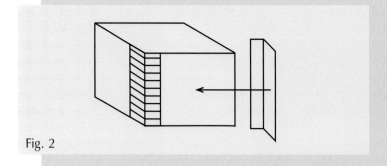

Fig. 2

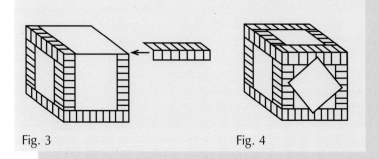

Fig. 3                    Fig. 4

10. Using hot-glue gun, adhere buttons onto top and sides of box as desired.

11. Using marking pen, write "buttons hold my coat together . . ." on one blank side of box and "but you keep me warm inside" on remaining side.

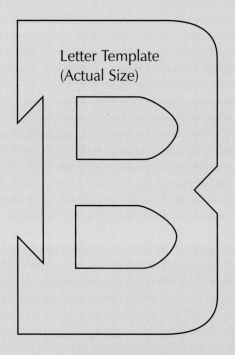

Letter Template
(Actual Size)

34

## Corrugated Candle Wrap

For gift giving or personal pleasure, this candle wrap is easily assembled for a look of simple elegance. Start by stacking two tea lights and then cutting a long strip of corrugated paper to their combined height. Wrap the paper tightly around the tea lights and glue to secure in place. Complete the look with a scrap of organza ribbon.

*Additional Supplies for Pastel Block:*
• Colored card stock: contrasting, 8½" x 11" (2)

*Additional Instructions for Pastel Block:*
1. Following Instructions for Basic Block on page 33, make block from card stock.

2. Cut two 3½" squares from first colored card stock and four squares from second colored card stock.

3. Glue squares from first card stock onto top and bottom of block.

4. Glue squares from second card stock onto four sides of block.

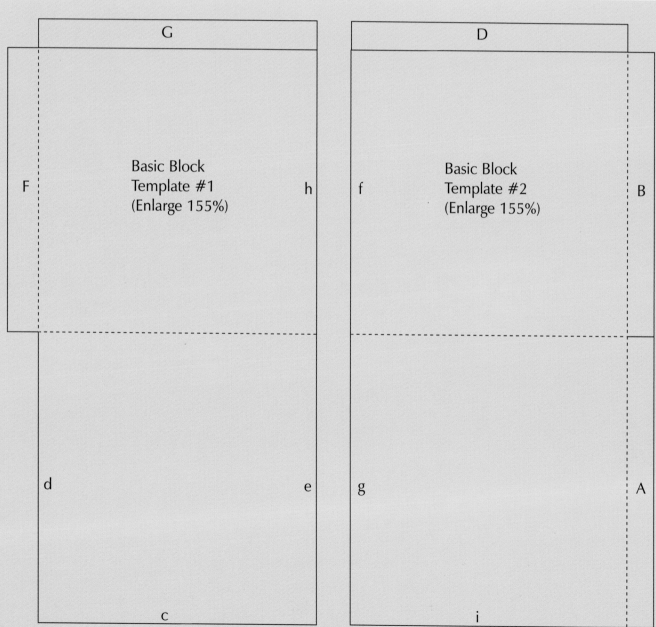

G

Basic Block
Template #1
(Enlarge 155%)

F                                    h

d                                    e

c

D

Basic Block
Template #2
(Enlarge 155%)

f                                    B

g                                    A

i

I

a

H

Basic Block
Template #3
(Enlarge 155%)

g

E

C

# Wooden Oriental Frame

## Supplies:
- Acrylic paints: terra-cotta; black
- All-purpose sealer
- Cotton cloth
- Craft knife
- Gel stain: oak
- Matte acrylic spray
- Paintbrush: flat
- Paper: oriental writings, 8½" x 11"
- Paper toweling
- Paraffin wax
- Sanding pad: fine grit
- Unfinished wooden picture frame with 3½" x 5" opening

*Instructions:*

1. Sand wood frame until edges and front are very smooth.

2. Spray front, sides, and back of frame with matte acrylic spray. Allow to dry.

3. Paint sides, back, and inside edges of frame with two coats of black, allowing to dry between coats.

4. Lightly rub paraffin on edges and in several places on sides where black paint should show through.

5. Paint front, sides, and inside edges with terra-cotta. If necessary, apply a second coat. Allow to dry.

6. Place frame on paper. Trace and cut out around frame and inside opening.

7. Refer to Fig. 1. Brush all-purpose sealer onto front of frame. Place cut-out paper with right side up onto frame. Using cloth, smooth paper onto sealer.

8. Immediately brush sealer on top of paper. Allow to dry.

9. Refer to Fig. 2. Using sanding pad, scuff off paint and paraffin wax around frame edges. Note: You may even remove some of the paper around the edges of the frame.

10. Brush gel stain onto front of frame. Using paper toweling, wipe off excess stain. Allow to dry.

11. Spray frame with matte acrylic spray. Allow to dry.

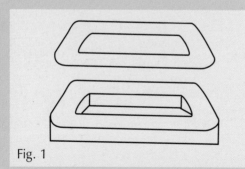

Fig. 1

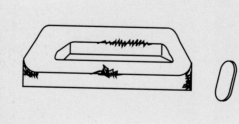

Fig. 2

# Lamp Shades

designed by David Dibble

*Supplies for Oval or Round Lamp Shade:*
• Oval or round lamp shade
• Paper: large enough to cover lampshade
• Paper scissors
• Spray adhesive

*Instructions Oval or Round Lamp Shade:*
1. Place paper with wrong side up on work surface. Roll lamp shade over paper to make certain it will cover properly.

2. Remove any fabric borders or decorations from lamp shade so it is as smooth and flat as possible.

3. Spray outside of lamp shade with spray adhesive.

4. Place lamp shade on paper and firmly roll until lamp shade surface is covered, slightly overlapping edges.

5. Trim paper to lamp shade, adding 2"–3" at bottom and top.

6. Lightly spray underside of paper with spray adhesive. Wrap paper to inside of lamp shade.

*Supplies for Square Lamp Shade:*
• Paper: large enough to cover lamp shade
• Paper scissors
• Pencil
• Spray adhesive
• Square lamp shade

*Instructions for Square Lamp Shade:*
1. Place paper with wrong side up on work surface.

2. Using lamp shade for pattern, place one side on paper. Trace and cut out paper, adding 2"–3" at bottom and top. Repeat for four sides.

40

3. Spray outside of lamp shade with spray adhesive.

4. Adhere one paper onto each side of lamp shade.

5. Lightly spray underside of paper with spray adhesive. Wrap paper to inside of lamp shade.

*Supplies for Embellished Lamp Shade:*
• Paper-covered lamp shade
• Tacky glue
• Tin shape

*Instructions for Embellished Lamp Shade:*
1. Glue tin shape onto covered lamp shade.

41

# Wire/Paper
## Black-and-White Flowers

*Supplies:*
- Craft wire: black
- Magazine pages: black-and-white images on one side
- Paper scissors
- White craft glue
- Wire cutters

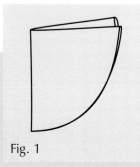

Fig. 1

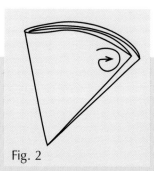

Fig. 2

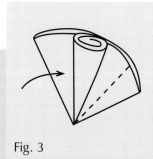

Fig. 3

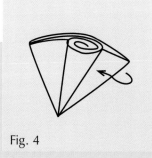

Fig. 4

*Instructions:*

1. Using wire cutters, cut five lengths of wire, varying from 9"–18" in length and set aside.

2. Using scissors, cut 2¾"-diameter circle from magazine page.

3. Refer to Fig. 1. Fold circle in half, then in half again.

4. Refer to Fig. 2. To form paper flower, roll one folded end toward opposite end, forming small cone at center.

5. Refer to Fig. 3. Tack cone to middle of remaining folded end with tiny amount of glue.

6. Refer to Fig. 4 and Folding on page 7. Fold remaining end, making a valley fold, about ½" from outer edge of quarter-circle shape.

7. Repeat Steps 2–6 to make 20 paper flowers and set aside.

8. Cut five 2½" squares from magazine pages.

9. Refer to Fig 5. To form origami frog, fold one square in half. Fold in half again, making smaller square.

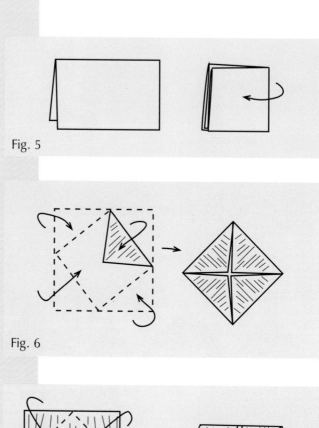

Fig. 5

10. Refer to Fig 6. Open square and place black-and-white images side down on work surface. Using fold lines as guide lines, fold all four corners inward, touching at center.

11. Turn folded square over so images side is up on work surface. Refer to Fig. 7. Fold corners inward, touching at center.

Fig. 6

12. Refer to Fig. 8 and Fig. 9. Turn square over again and open center flaps, allowing paper to fold in diagonal direction, while you insert your fingers and make four little cups. Note: As you continue folding the paper backward, the "mountain" sides of the frog will touch center.

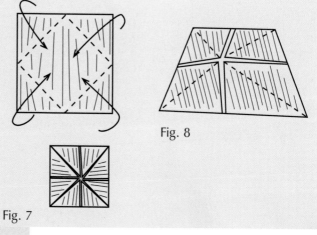

Fig. 8

Fig. 7

13. Refer to Fig. 10. Apply a small amount of craft glue to images side at tips of little cups. Place origami frog onto tip of wire and firmly push tips together. Allow to dry.

14. Insert one paper flower into each "cup" of frog, with rolled cone toward outside. Glue in place.

15. Place flowers in appropriate vase.

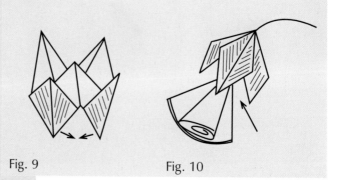

Fig. 9                    Fig. 10

# Paper Shelf Liner

*Supplies:*
- Paper punches: diamond; round
- Decorative-edged scissors: mini scallop; ripple
- Newspapers
- Paper scissors

*Instructions:*

1. Refer to Fig. 1. Fold newspaper in half and in half again. Continue folding in this manner until paper is about 1¾" wide.

2. Refer to Fig. 2. Using paper scissors, cut paper to width of shelf plus 2"–2½".

3. Refer to Fig. 3. Using decorative-edged scissors, cut raw edges in a scalloped or triangular shape.

4. Refer to Fig. 4. Punch holes to echo cut edge.

5. Unfold newspaper and line storage shelves.

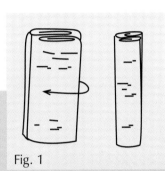

Fig. 1

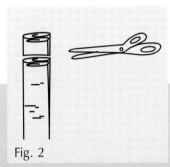

Fig. 2

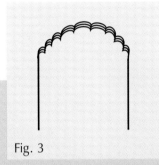

Fig. 3

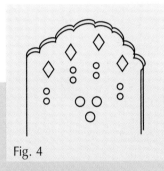

Fig. 4

## Paper Border

A decorative paper border is an old-fashioned way to add a new touch of sophistication to many otherwise ordinary pieces. This cake pedestal is embellished with a paper border made from newspaper in much the same manner as is the Paper Shelf Liner pictured on page 45.

# Paper Light Cover

**Supplies:**
- Acrylic paint: terra-cotta
- Balsa wood: 1"-wide, 6'
- Coping saw
- Drill and ¹⁄₁₆" drill bit
- Floor can light
- Handmade paper: 36" square
- L-shaped brackets: ½"-wide x 1"-long (16)
- Paintbrush: flat
- Paper scissors
- Pencil
- Ruler
- White craft glue
- Wood screws: ⅛"-diameter x ½" (32)
- Wooden dowels: ½"-square x 36" (6)

**Instructions:**

1. Using saw, cut eight 9" pieces from two dowels for stabilizers.

2. Drill small holes for screw placement.

3. Refer to Fig. 1. Attach one L-shaped bracket onto one side of each end of stabilizers, placing corner of "L" flush with end.

4. Measure and mark 2" from each end of remaining 36" dowels.

5. Refer to Fig. 2. Attach one 9" stabilizer at each mark and perpendicular to one dowel, with L-shaped brackets facing each other.

6. Refer to Fig. 3. Attach another dowel to remaining end of stabilizers.

7. Repeat Steps 5–6 for two remaining dowels.

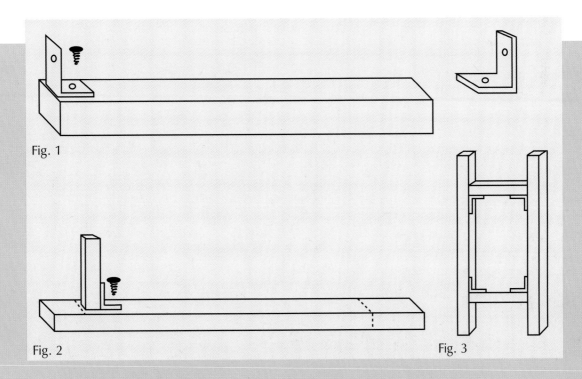

Fig. 1

Fig. 2

Fig. 3

8. Refer to Fig. 4. Place completed front and back frames on a table facing you. Measure and mark 2½" from each end of four dowels.

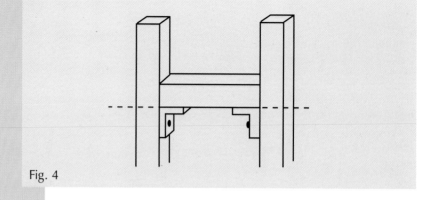

Fig. 4

9. Refer to Fig. 5. Attach remaining 9" stabilizers at marks and perpendicular to dowels, creating frame.

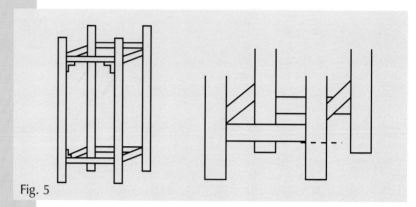

Fig. 5

10. Refer to Fig. 6. Wrap and glue paper around frame, overlapping beginning edge.

11. Measure width of each side, and cut eight pieces from balsa wood accordingly.

12. Paint wood pieces with terracotta. Allow to dry.

13. Refer to Fig. 7. Glue wood pieces onto top and bottom edges of paper, creating light cover.

14. Center light cover over a floor can light.

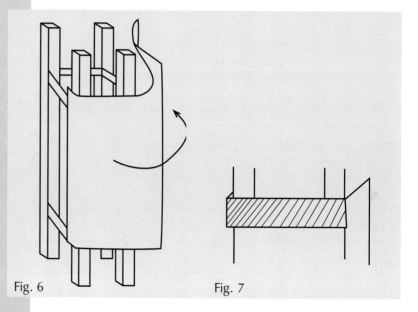

Fig. 6          Fig. 7

*Apothecary Jar Labels*

Antique bottles, junk store glassware, and old cast-off jars can create an eclectic display of your favorite things—simply by adding your own labels. Photocopy the Apothecary Jar Label Patterns on opposite page onto soft shades of colored card stock—or try designing your own. Fill jars with bath and kitchen necessities like herbs, spices, vitamins, or bath salts or use them to display a treasured collection of buttons, beads, or shells.

Apothecary Jar Label Patterns
(Actual Size)

**CALCIUM**

Calcium Carbonate

500 mg.

*Chamomile*

*M. chamomilia*

4 ounces

*Echinacea*

Made in France

# German Christmas Bells

*Supplies:*
- Brown kraft paper
- Glitter spray
- Needle and metallic thread
- Paper scissors
- Pencil
- Ruler
- White craft glue

*Instructions:*
1. Cut a 8¾" square from kraft paper.

2. Refer to Fig. 1. Fold square in half, then in half again. Open square.

3. Refer to Fig. 2. Fold diagonally, corner to corner, then repeat for remaining corners. Open square again.

4. Refer to Fig. 3. Fold from corner to midway mark on opposite side of square. Fold from opposite corner to midway mark on opposite side of square.

5. Refer to Fig. 4. Repeat Step 4 around all four sides of square.

6. Refer to Fig. 5 and Fig. 6. Fold center of each side inward on all four sides. Note: As you begin to push in the center areas, the corners will also begin to fold up until all four corners touch.

7. Tack inside folds of bell with tiny amount of glue and press together until glue sets up.

8. Using needle, take metallic thread through top end of bell. Tie ends of thread together in a knot 3"–4" from top of bell for a hanger.

9. Spray bells with gold or silver glitter spray.

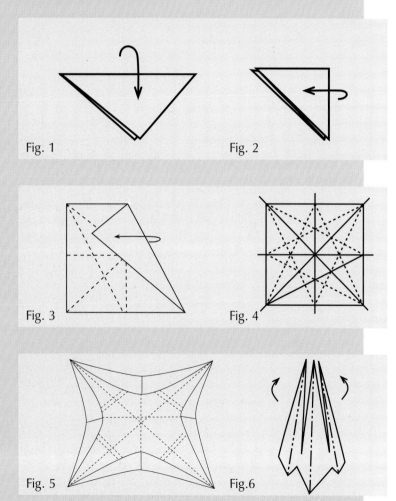

Fig. 1

Fig. 2

Fig. 3

Fig. 4

Fig. 5

Fig.6

# Paper Balls

*Supplies for Basic Ball:*
- Aluminum foil: approximately 5'
- Craft scissors
- Metallic thread
- Paper of choice to cover ball
- White craft glue

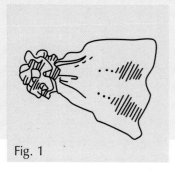

Fig. 1

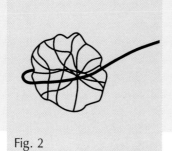

Fig. 2

*Instructions for Basic Ball:*

1. Refer to Fig. 1. Pull off 12"–18" sections of foil and form into a firm, but not completely compact ball shape. Note: Avoid using excess pressure on the foil or you will use too much foil.

2. Cover foil ball with selected paper.

3. Refer to Fig. 2. Wrap metallic thread around covered ball, in all directions, until paper is secured to ball. Note: Thread should be wrapped firmly but not too tightly, or thread might break.

4. Cut metallic thread. Glue thread end onto ball. Note: If you have difficulty keeping the thread end in place until it is dry, insert a straight pin into the ball and wrap the thread around it twice to hold it in place while the glue is drying. The glue will dry clear.

*Wrapping Paper Ball:*
   Inexpensive wrapping papers in shades of taupe, cream, and light moss green were used to cover the basic ball on opposite page. It was then wrapped with copper thread.

*Tissue/Handmade Paper Ball:*
   The basic ball was covered with dark pine green tissue paper and wrapped part way with a small piece of blue handmade paper. It was completed by wrapping it with gold thread.

*Tissue Paper & Leaf Ball:*
   Shimmery gold tissue paper covers the basic ball. The ball was then wrapped with silver thread as, one at a time, moss green silk leaves were added in.

## Japanese Helmets

*Supplies:*
- Colored paper: 8½" x 11"
- Paper scissors or craft knife
- Pencil
- Ruler

*Instructions:*

1. Refer to Fig. 1. Cut an 8½" square from colored paper. Fold square in half, diagonally.

2. Refer to Fig. 2. Bring each folded corner to the center at a right angle.

3. Refer to Fig. 3. Fold lower corners upward.

4. Refer to Fig. 4. Fold corners, which were just folded upward, outward. Note: The fold begins about ¼" at the top center and ends at the middle of the square.

5. Refer to Fig. 5. Fold one layer of bottom corner upward, with fold line ½" below center line.

6. Refer to Fig. 6. Fold edge upward again.

7. Refer to Fig. 7. Fold side corners toward back, ⅜" from edges.

8. Refer to Fig. 8. Turn helmet over and fold up remaining triangle. Open helmet slightly so it will stand.

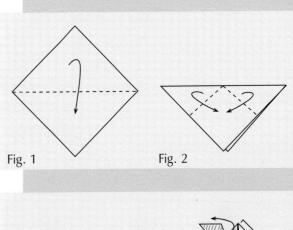

Fig. 1        Fig. 2

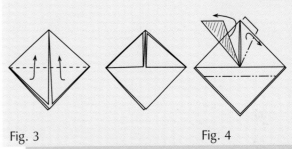

Fig. 3        Fig. 4

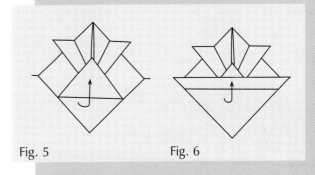

Fig. 5        Fig. 6

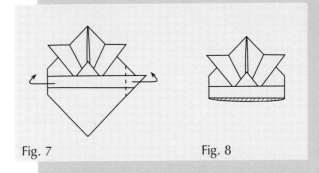

Fig. 7        Fig. 8

## Magazine Woven Heart

*Supplies:*
- Dried roses
- Magazine pages: black-and-white print (1); colored images (1)
- Paper scissors
- Pencil
- Ruler
- White craft glue

*Instructions:*

Note: Refer to Fig. 1. For instruction purposes, one color of paper is referred to as "A" and the other as "B." The weaving rows are designated by numbers. Therefore, 1A means Row 1, Paper A and so forth.

1. Photocopy Woven Hearts Template on opposite page. Cut out copied template.

2. Fold each magazine page in half. Place template on fold. Trace and cut one heart piece from each folded magazine page. Cut along lines as indicated on template.

3. Refer to Fig. 2. Begin weaving 1B into 1A.

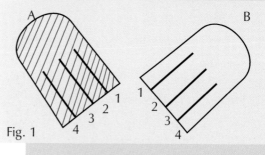

Fig. 1

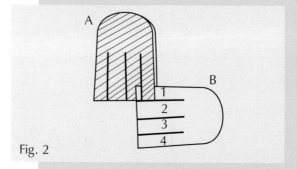

Fig. 2

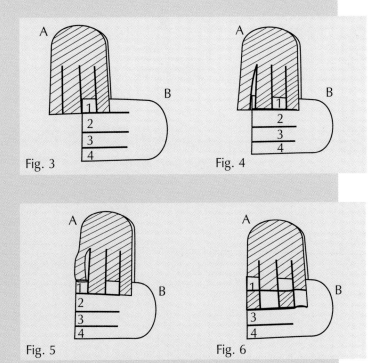

Fig. 3

Fig. 4

Fig. 5

Fig. 6

Woven Hearts Template
(Enlarge 110%)

place on fold

4. Refer to Fig. 3. Lift 2A up, and as you continue pushing 1B further, insert 2A into 1B.

5. Refer to Fig. 4. Insert 1B into 3A.

6. Refer to Fig. 5. As 1B exits 3A, lift up 4A and insert into 1B. One row of weaving is now complete.

7. Refer to Fig. 6. Carefully slide 1B upward to prepare for weaving 2B.

8. Insert 1A into 2B.

9. Insert 2B into 2A, and so forth until 2B is woven into the row.

10. Continue sliding weaving upward and repeating weaving pattern of the first two rows to complete the heart.

11. Glue dried roses and leaves onto finished heart.

## Brown Paper Package & Button Gift Tag

Turn ordinary into extraordinary by drawing swirls onto plain brown paper with a metallic paint pen and topping your package with a sparkling ribbon. The charming gift tag was made by photocopying and tracing the Basic Tag Templates on page 78 onto two pieces of contrasting colored card stock. Punch a hole in the top and join them together with a scrap of ribbon. Buttons from your sewing jar, elegant charms, or even tiny seashells can be glued onto the top tag, leaving the bottom tag for your special message.

# Gift Box Ornament

**Supplies:**
- Colored card stock: taupe, 8½" x 11"
- Paper glue
- Paper scissors
- Pencil

**Instructions:**

1. Photocopy Gift Box Ornament Template. Cut out copied template.

2. Using template, trace and cut triangle from colored card stock.

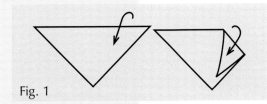

Fig. 1

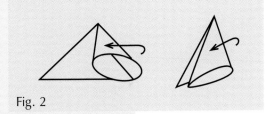

Fig. 2

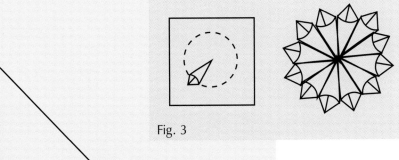

Fig. 3

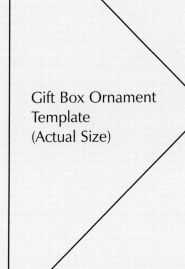

Gift Box Ornament
Template
(Actual Size)

Fig. 4

Fig. 5

3. Refer to Fig. 1. Place triangle on work surface with flat side of triangle up and point toward front. Fold right point down at a 45° angle.

4. Refer to Fig. 2. Roll toward left point until all points are together to form a cone.

5. Tack points of cone with tiny amount of glue.

6. Repeat Steps 2–5 to make 12 cones.

7. Refer to Fig. 3. Determine center of wrapped gift box. Glue each cone to box with pointed ends touching at center and forming a circle.

8. Refer to Fig. 4. Cut a ¼"-wide strip from card stock. Beginning at one end, roll strip to create a coil.

9. Refer to Fig. 5. Glue coil onto center of cone arrangement.

A SUDDEN SUMMER SHO

# Lacy Gift Pockets

## Supplies:
- Colored card stock: 8½" x 11"
- Double-sided tape
- Magazine pages: colored images, 8½" x 11" (3)
- Paper doily: 6"-diameter
- Paper glue
- Silk ribbon scrap
- Wire-edged ribbon scrap

## Instructions for Large Gift Pocket:

1. Cut two 7½" x 8" pieces from two magazine pages.

2. Refer to Fig. 1. Fold long edges of each cut page in ⅝".

3. Refer to Fig. 2. Attach double-sided tape onto folded edges and bottom edge of one cut page.

4. Refer to Fig. 3. Remove protective covering from tape and carefully place remaining cut page, with wrong sides together, on top of first page.

5. Refer to Fig. 4. Fold paper doily in half. Place fold over top of pocket. Glue wrong side of doily onto back side of pocket.

6. Tie a bow in silk ribbon. Center and glue bow onto front edge of doily.

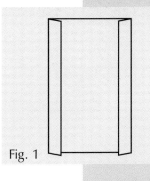

Fig. 1

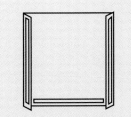

Fig. 2

Fig. 3

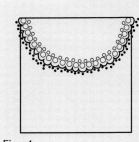

Fig. 4

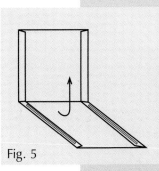

Fig. 5

## Instructions for Small Gift Pocket:

1. Cut a 7½" x 11" piece from one magazine page.

2. Fold long edges of cut page in ⅝".

3. Fold page in half widthwise.

4. Refer to Fig. 5. Unfold and attach double-sided tape onto lower folded edges.

5. Remove protective covering from tape and carefully fold page again.

6. Cut a 3½" x 5" rectangle from colored card stock. Trim short edges in a scallop design for a handmade doily.

7. Repeat Steps 5–6 for Instructions for Large Gift Pocket with handmade doily and wire-edged ribbon.

Tip: Wrap the gift in a piece of tissue paper to keep any sharp edges from protruding through the gift pocket.

# Windmill Weave Card

designed by David Dibble

*Supplies:*
- Colored card stock: contrasting, 8½" x 11" (7)
- Craft knife
- Paper glue
- Pencil
- Ruler

*Instructions:*

1. Cut a 6½" square from one piece of card stock.

2. Center and draw a horizontal and vertical line on one side, dividing square in half both ways.

3. Cut a 3¼" x 9¾" strip each from four different colors of card stock.

4. Glue one end of each strip onto 6½" square from each side, using pencil lines for placement to form a windmill pattern.

5. Cut two 6" squares from two coordinating pieces of card stock. Note: These squares will be used for writing messages.

6. Turn windmill over with 6½" square up on work surface. Fold remaining end of each strip over so it lays flat across square.

7. Open folded strips. Place message squares on top of 6½" square. Sequentially fold each strip again enclosing message squares within. Tuck in end of last strip to create a woven effect.

Mrs. Marguerite Christensen
RFD Box 167
Antonito, CO 81120

33 USA

# Torn-Paper
## Note Card & Envelope

*Supplies:*
- Colored card stock: coordinating, 8½" x 11"
- Colored papers: contrasting, 8½" x 11" (3)
- Decorative-edged scissors: ripple
- Double-sided tape: narrow with protective covering
- Fine-tipped marking pen: black
- Paper glue
- Paper scissors
- Pencil
- Ruler

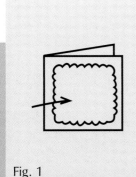

Fig. 1

Fig. 2

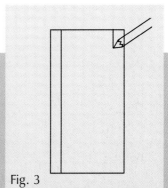

Fig. 3

*Instructions:*

1. Using paper scissors, cut a 5" x 10" rectangle from colored paper. Fold rectangle in half for a 5" square card.

2. Refer to Fig. 1. Using pencil, draw a 4½" square onto card stock. Using decorative-edged scissors, cut out square. Center and glue square onto front of card.

3. Photocopy Note Card Templates on page 68. Using paper scissors, cut out copied templates.

4. Using template and pencil, trace selected shape onto contrasting colored paper.

5. Refer to Fig. 2. Tear around traced shape. Center and glue torn shape onto front of card, with traced side down.

6. Using fine-tipped marking pen, draw border design as desired.

7. Using paper scissors, cut a 5¾" x 11" rectangle from colored paper to make envelope.

8. Refer to Fig. 3. Using pencil, draw lines ¼" in along 11" edges of rectangle.

9. Refer to Fig. 4. Fold ½" in from 5¾" edge for top flap. Fold remainder of rectangle in half up to flap fold. Unfold.

10. Refer to Fig. 5. Using paper scissors, trim along lines on 11" edges of rectangle, from top edge down to main fold.

11. Refer to Fig. 6. Fold side edges in on lines.

12. Apply glue to folded edges. Fold upper portion over onto glue. Press and allow to dry.

13. Refer to Fig. 7. Attach double-sided tape along top edge. Note: Leave the protective covering on tape until ready to seal the envelope.

Tip: Try using this technique for creating scrap-book pages.

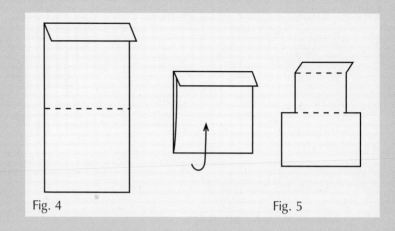

Fig. 4　　　　　　　　　　　　　　Fig. 5

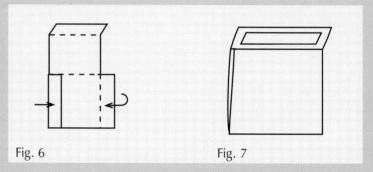

Fig. 6　　　　　　　　　Fig. 7

Note Card Templates (Actual Size)

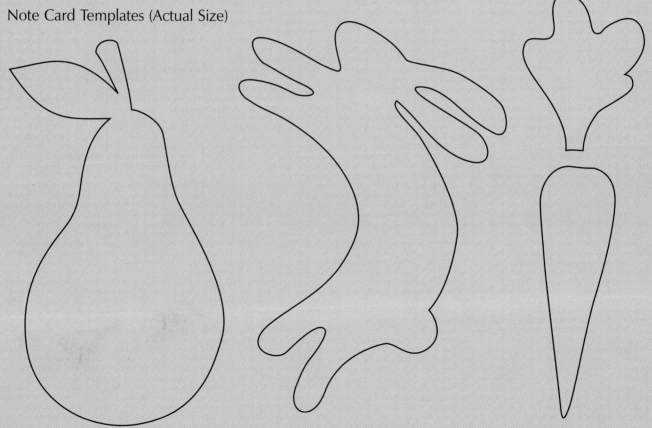

## Coffee Pouch

This flavorful package is actually an invitation to a long overdue get-together and a cup of coffee. Photocopy and trace the Coffee Pouch Template on pages 70–71 onto highly textured handmade paper. Fold and glue as indicated, then fill with a favorite blend of fresh roasted coffee beans. An invitation was placed on the front and a folded book of coffee recipes dangles from the cinch. This delightful package gives new meaning to the phrase, "aroma therapy."

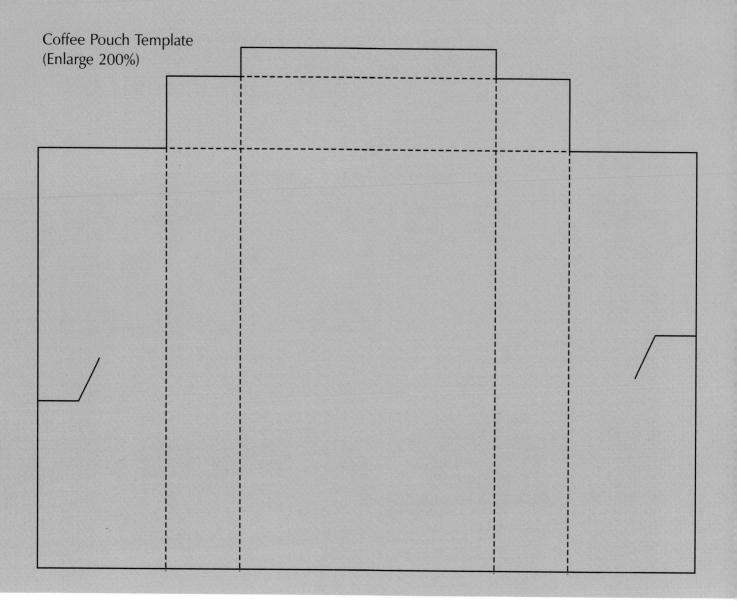

Coffee Pouch Template
(Enlarge 200%)

*Instructions for Recipe Book:*
1. Photocopy the Coffee Pouch Recipe Book Patterns on opposite page onto colored card stock.

2. Refer to Fig. 1–3 to fold each square. Refer to Fig. 4 to glue the two folded squares together.

3. Refer to Fig. 5 to glue one 2" square of cardboard onto opposite sides of each folded square.

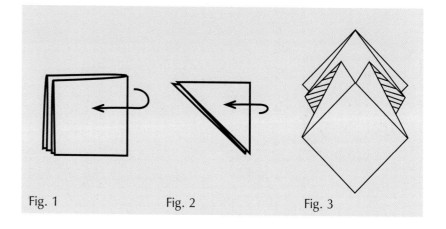

Fig. 1          Fig. 2          Fig. 3

70

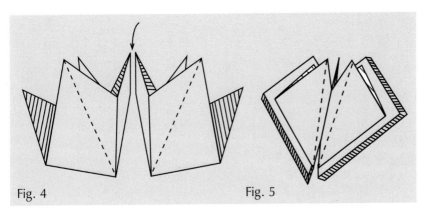

Fig. 4          Fig. 5

*Instructions for Gift Tag & Invitation:*

1. Photocopy the Coffee Pouch Gift Tag and Invitation Patterns below onto contrasting colored card stock.

2. Glue the Gift Tag onto front of the recipe book.

3. Glue the invitation onto front of the coffee pouch.

Coffee Pouch Recipe Book, Invitation, & Gift Tag Patterns (Actual Size)

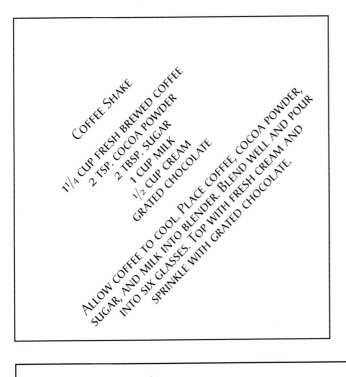

COFFEE SHAKE

1¼ CUP FRESH BREWED COFFEE
2 TSP. COCOA POWDER
2 TBSP. SUGAR
1 CUP MILK
½ CUP CREAM
GRATED CHOCOLATE

ALLOW COFFEE TO COOL. PLACE COFFEE, COCOA POWDER, SUGAR, AND MILK INTO BLENDER. BLEND WELL AND POUR INTO SIX GLASSES. TOP WITH FRESH CREAM AND SPRINKLE WITH GRATED CHOCOLATE.

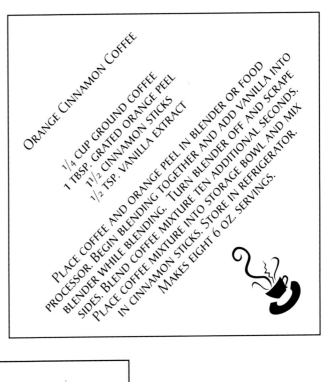

ORANGE CINNAMON COFFEE

¼ CUP GROUND COFFEE
1 TBSP. GRATED ORANGE PEEL
1½ CINNAMON STICKS
½ TSP. VANILLA EXTRACT

PLACE COFFEE AND ORANGE PEEL IN BLENDER OR FOOD PROCESSOR. BEGIN BLENDING. TURN BLENDER OFF AND ADD VANILLA INTO BLENDER WHILE BLENDING. TURN BLENDER OFF AND SCRAPE SIDES. BLEND COFFEE MIXTURE TEN ADDITIONAL SECONDS. PLACE COFFEE MIXTURE INTO STORAGE BOWL AND MIX IN CINNAMON STICKS. STORE IN REFRIGERATOR. MAKES EIGHT 6 OZ. SERVINGS.

*Have Coffee With Me!*

EVERYTIME WE MEET WE SAY, "LET'S GET TOGETHER SOON."

I THINK IT MUST BE "SOON."

WHEN: _____ AT _____

WHERE: _____

IT IS AROUND THE TABLE THAT FRIENDS UNDERSTAND THE WARMTH OF BEING TOGETHER.
OLD ITALIAN SAYING

CALL ME SOON: _____

EXPECTANTLY YOURS, _____

For:

# Bird's Nest Candleholder

**Instructions:**

1. Glue card stock onto cover stock. Allow to dry.

2. Photocopy Star Template. Cut out copied template.

3. Place template on silver card stock. Trace and cut out star.

4. Flatten bottom of wire bird's nest. Center and glue nest onto silver side of star. Allow to dry.

5. Place votive cup into nest.

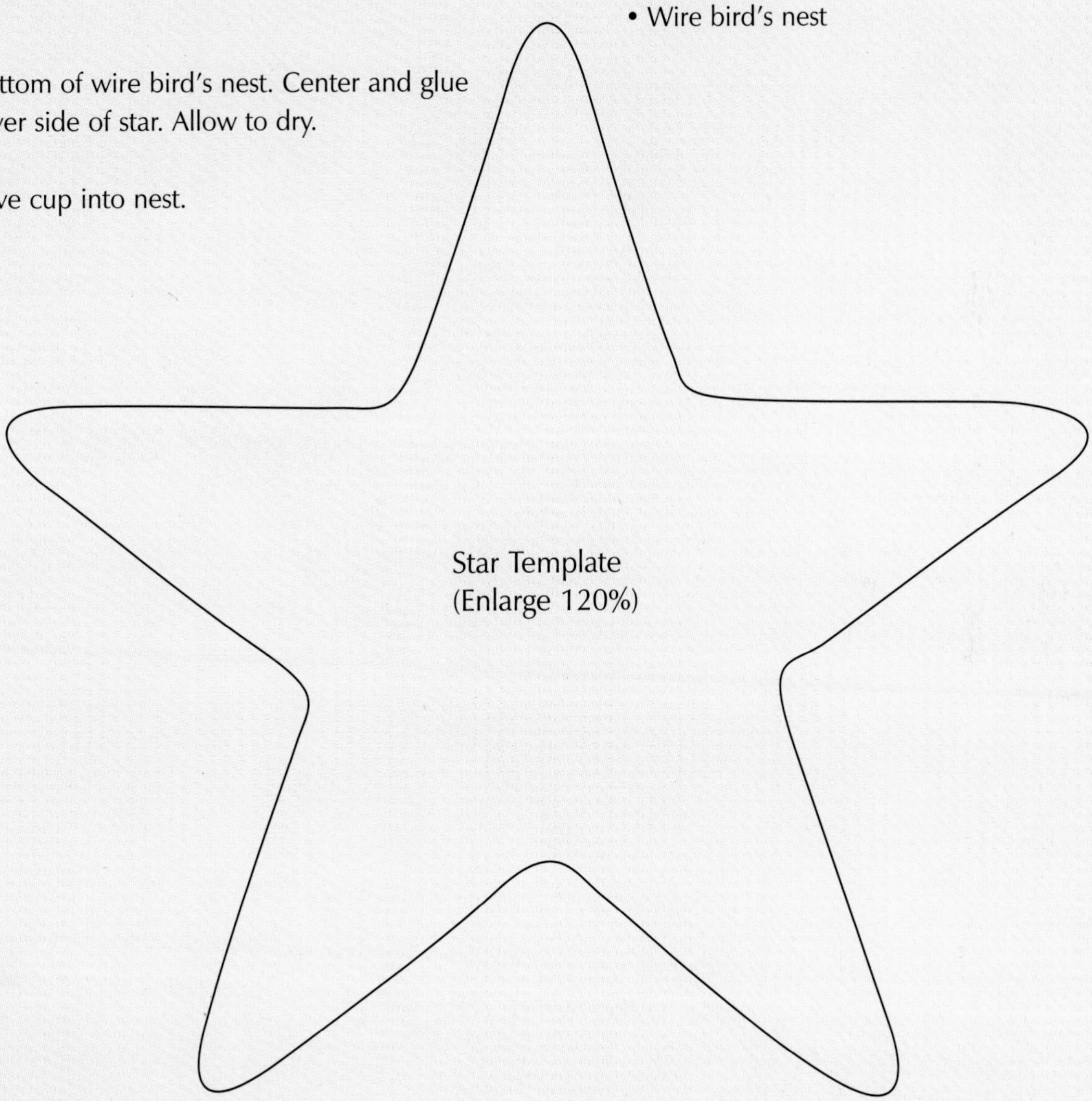

**Supplies:**
- Card stock: silver, 8½" x 11"
- Cover stock: white, 8½" x 11"
- Craft glue
- Paper scissors
- Pencil
- Votive cup
- Wire bird's nest

Star Template
(Enlarge 120%)

# Leaf Card

designed by David Dibble

*Supplies:*
- Card stock: off-white, 9" x 15"
- Craft knife
- Decoupage glue
- Handmade paper: fibrous, 8½" x 11" (3)
- Pencil
- Pressed leaf
- Ruler

*Instructions:*

1. Photocopy Leaf Card Template. Cut out copied template.

2. Using template, trace and cut leaf card from off-white card stock.

3. Fold card as indicated.

4. Glue pressed leaf onto front of card.

5. Cut 24 3¼" x 7½" rectangles from hand-made paper and place them inside folded card. Note: These rectangles will be used for writing messages.

Leaf Card Template
(Enlarge 190%)

Note: The delicate oval box pictured with the Leaf Card is also made of paper. It was purchased at a specialty store and its maker is unknown.

## Tree Tag

Add a handmade touch to purchased bags and wrappings to convey to your friends that they must be very special indeed. Turn a simple shape cut from card stock into a one-of-a-kind tag by stitching it onto a scrap of handmade paper with metallic thread and then carefully tearing around the edges. Punch a hole through the top, add a ribbon, and it is ready for your personalized message. A template for the Tree Tag has been included on page 78, but try experimenting with different shapes to make your package perfect for any occasion.

# Doorknob Card

designed by David Dibble

*Instructions:*

1. Cut a 3½" x 8½" rectangle from brown card stock. Cut a 3" square from green card stock.

2. Photocopy Leaf Template below and Doorknob Card Template on page 78. Cut out copied templates.

3. Using leaf template, trace and cut leaf from handmade paper. Using pocket template, trace and cut pocket from green card stock.

4. Score and fold pocket as indicated, and glue onto bottom of brown rectangle.

5. Turn rectangle over. Center and place leaf and green square on top of brown rectangle. Using small paper punch, center and punch a hole through all three pieces. String a piece of twine through holes and tie in a knot.

6. Using large paper punch, punch a hole through each top corner. Tie a loop of twine, large enough to hang on a doorknob, through holes.

7. Cut four 2¾" x 7" rectangles from speckled paper. Place rectangles in pocket. Note: These rectangles will be used for writing messages.

*Supplies:*
- Bone folder or butter knife
- Colored card stock: brown, 8½" x 11"; green, 8½" x 11"
- Craft knife
- Handmade paper: grass, 8½" x 11"
- Paper: speckled, 8½" x 11"
- Paper glue
- Paper punches: large round; small round
- Pencil
- Ruler
- Twine

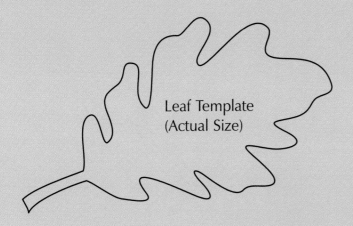

Leaf Template
(Actual Size)

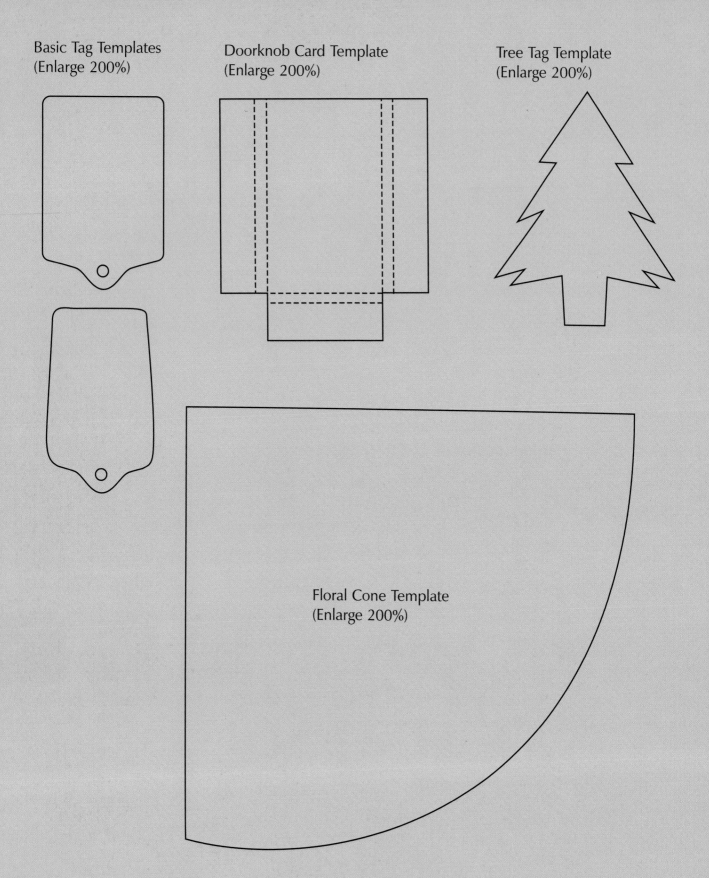

Basic Tag Templates
(Enlarge 200%)

Doorknob Card Template
(Enlarge 200%)

Tree Tag Template
(Enlarge 200%)

Floral Cone Template
(Enlarge 200%)

# Floral Cone & Circular Fan

*Supplies:*
- Handmade papers: brown, 12" x 12"; floral, 12" x 12" (2); tan, 12" x 12"
- Paper glue
- Pencil
- Pressed leaf
- Ruler

*Instructions for Floral Cone:*

1. Photocopy Floral Cone Template on page 78. Using scissors, cut out copied template.

2. Using template, trace and cut cone from tan paper. Gently curve paper to form a cone. Note: Take care to avoid bending the paper.

3. Overlap straight edges and glue in place.

4. Refer to Fig. 1. Cut three 1" strips from brown paper and glue together for 36" strip. Accordion-fold strip with ½" folds.

5. Glue folded strip onto top ½" of cone edge, overlapping short edges at back of cone.

6. Glue pressed leaf onto brown paper. Wet paper around edges of leaf. Tear wet paper around leaf.

7. Cut three ¼" x 8½" strips from brown paper. Beginning at one end, roll each strip to create a coil.

8. Glue leaf and coils onto cone.

*Instructions for Circular Fan:*

1. Refer to Figs. 1–2. Accordion-fold floral papers with 1" folds and fold each in half to create a fan shape. Glue folds together at center and where ends meet to hold fan in place. Glue fans together to create a circular fan.

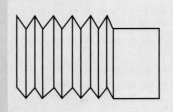

Fig. 1

Fig. 2

# Sunflower Card

designed by David Dibble

*Supplies:*
- Craft knife
- Card stock: coordinating, 12" x 12" (2)
- Handmade paper: highly textured, 8½" x 11"
- Paper punch: small round
- Pencil
- Ruler
- Twine

*Instructions:*

1. Cut a 6" x 12" rectangle from each piece of card stock. Cut a 6" square from handmade paper.

2. Place darker piece of card stock on top of lighter piece. Fold both pieces as one in half for a card. Open card and separate pieces.

3. Photocopy Flower Templates. Cut out copied templates.

### Flower Templates
(Enlarge 200%)

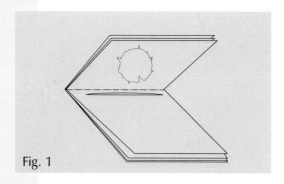

Fig. 1

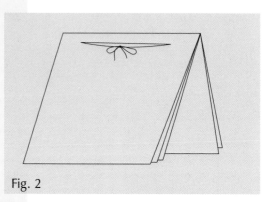

Fig. 2

4. Using larger flower template, center and trace flower onto front of darker piece of card stock. Using smaller flower template, center and trace flower onto front of lighter piece of card stock. Using craft knife, cut out flowers.

5. Refer to Fig. 1. Place pieces of card stock together and place handmade paper square within card.

6. Using paper punch, punch two holes through handmade paper square and both pieces of card stock, near fold of card.

7. Refer to Fig. 2. Thread twine through holes and tie in back.

# Wine Holder

designed by Nicole Larsen

*Supplies:*
- Buttons
- Corrugated paper: 14" x 18"
- Craft knife
- Hot-glue gun and glue sticks
- Leather lacing
- Pencil
- Ruler
- Wooden circle: 4"-diameter

*Instructions:*

1. Photocopy Wine Holder Template. Cut out copied template.

2. Using template, trace and cut shape from corrugated paper.

3. Wrap and glue long straight edge of paper around sides of wooden circle, overlapping edges.

4. Glue buttons onto edge as desired.

5. Wrap leather lacing around buttons.

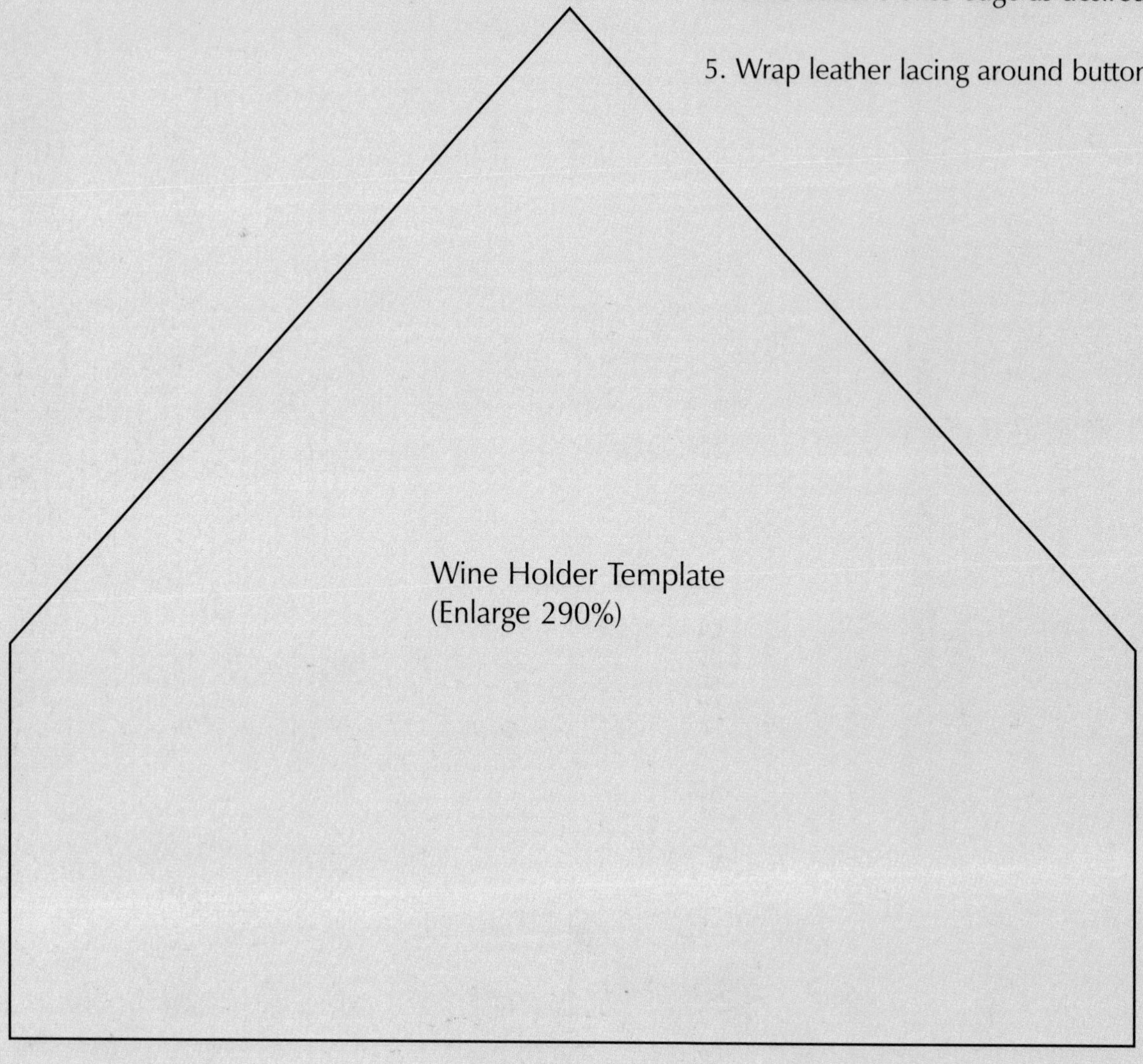

Wine Holder Template
(Enlarge 290%)

# Hand Card

designed by David Dibble

*Supplies:*
- Acrylic paint to match purchased box
- Craft knife
- Mat board: white, 10" square
- Paintbrush: flat
- Paper glue
- Pencil
- Purchased gift box with a base no larger than 2¾" square

*Instructions:*

1. Photocopy Hand Card Template. Cut out copied template.

2. Using template, trace and cut hand from mat board.

3. Paint hand with matching paint.

4. Glue bottom of gift box onto square area between fingers of hand. Put under pressure while first drying to ensure a flat and even bond. Note: Encyclopedias or rubber bands work well for this purpose.

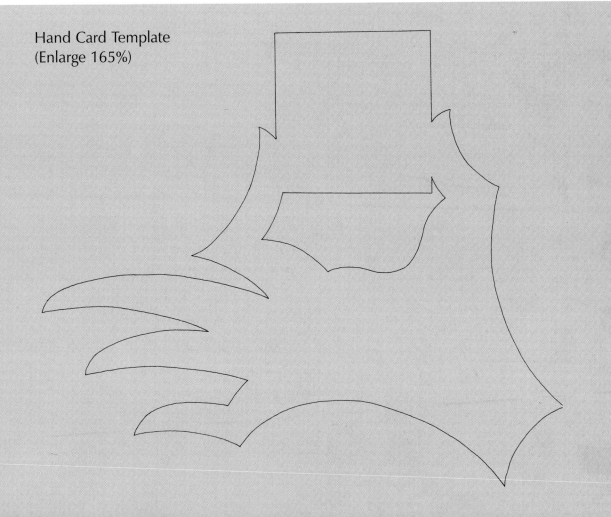

Hand Card Template
(Enlarge 165%)

# Santa Claus Card

designed by David Dibble

*Supplies:*
- Card stock: off-white, 8½" x 11"
- Cover stock: green, 6¾" x 13¾"
- Craft knife
- Handmade tissue paper: green, 8½" x 11"
- Paper: speckled, 8½" x 11"
- Paper punch: small round
- Pencil
- Ruler
- Stamp, photograph, or other art: 2" square
- Twine

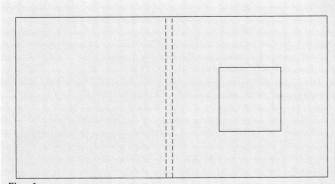

Fig. 1

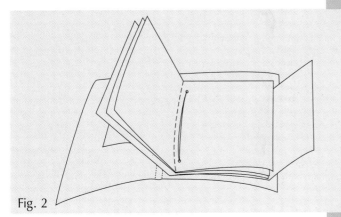

Fig. 2

*Instructions:*

1. Refer to Fig. 1. Center and cut a 2¾" square opening from one side of cover stock. Fold as indicated.

2. Cut a 6" x 10" rectangle from card stock. Cut two 5¾" x 9½" rectangles from speckled paper and one from handmade tissue paper. Fold each rectangle in half.

3. Place back sides of folded speckled papers within folded handmade tissue paper so that one opens right and the other left.

4. Center and place these papers within folded card stock with fold facing left. Place all of these together within folded cover stock ⅞" from fold.

5. Open all folds. Using paper punch, punch two holes through all pieces near fold of paper and card stock.

6. Refer to Fig. 2. Thread twine through holes and tie in back.

7. Stamp, draw, or glue art onto front of card stock within opening of cover stock.

# Clothesline Garland

*Supplies:*
- Fine-tipped marking pen: black
- Jute twine: 1 yard
- Miniature wooden clothespins (1 bag)
- Paper scissors
- Paper scraps, including black card stock
- Pencil
- Tacky glue

*Instructions:*

1. Photocopy Clothes Templates. Cut out copied templates.

2. Using templates, pencil, and scissors, trace and cut clothes pieces from various colors and patterns of paper scraps.

3. Glue clothes pieces onto contrasting colored papers.

4. Using marking pen, outline clothes pieces with a broken line. Draw in buttons and other details. Note: These details may be drawn in a carefree manner.

5. Make a knot in each end of jute twine. Attach paper clothes onto twine with miniature clothespins. If desired, mount "clothesline" on a board (painted or covered with paper) for display.

Clothes Templates (Actual Size)

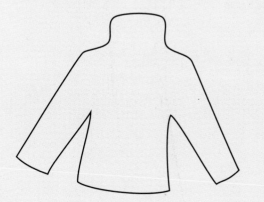

# Hanalee Scrapbook Page

*Supplies:*
- Alphabet beads
- Buttons
- Card stock: dark green, 8½" x 11"; light green, 8½" x 11"; medium green, 8½" x 11"; pale green, 8½" x 11"
- Decorative-edged scissors: mini pinking; mini scallop; pinking;
- Heavy-duty thread: green
- Needle
- Paper glue
- Paper scissors
- Photograph

*Instructions:*

1. Using paper scissors, cut a 1¾" x 3¾" rectangle from dark green card stock. Using mini scallop decorative-edged scissors, cut a 4¾" x 5⅝" rectangle from dark green card stock. Using pinking decorative-edged scissors, cut a 5¼" x 6¼" rectangle from medium green card stock. Using mini pinking decorative-edged scissors, cut a 6" x 7½" rectangle from light green card stock.

2. Center and glue larger dark green rectangle onto medium green rectangle. Center and glue medium green rectangle onto light green rectangle. Glue light green rectangle onto pale green card stock, centered from side to side and ½" from bottom edge.

3. Refer to photograph. Stitch across bottom and right side of light green rectangle as desired. Stitch "flower stems" across top of rectangle and attach buttons, in varying heights, for flower heads.

4. String beads onto thread to form name for book.

5. Place beads on front of smaller dark green rectangle and glue ends of thread onto back top corners.

6. Glue rectangle onto pale green card stock, centered from side to side and ½" from top edge.

7. Center and glue photograph onto center of larger dark green rectangle.

# Dimensional Ornaments

*Supplies:*
- Bone folder or butter knife
- Colored cover stock: 8½" x 11"
- Embroidery floss
- Needle
- Paper scissors
- Ruler
- White craft glue

*Instructions:*

1. Photocopy Dimensional Ornament Templates. Cut out copied templates.

2. Using template, trace and cut star and heart three times each from colored cover stock. Note: You can use the same color or vary the colors.

3. Refer to Fig. 1. Using bone folder or butter knife, score center of two of each shape.

4. Refer to Fig. 2. Fold one scored shape with a mountain fold and other with a valley fold, creating mirror images.

5. Refer to Fig. 3. Glue mountain fold onto center of flat shape, matching the outside edges.

6. Glue remaining folded shape onto remaining flat side, matching outside edges.

7. Refer to Fig. 4. Using needle, take embroidery floss through top of ornament. Tie ends of floss together in a knot 3"–4" from top of ornament for a hanger.

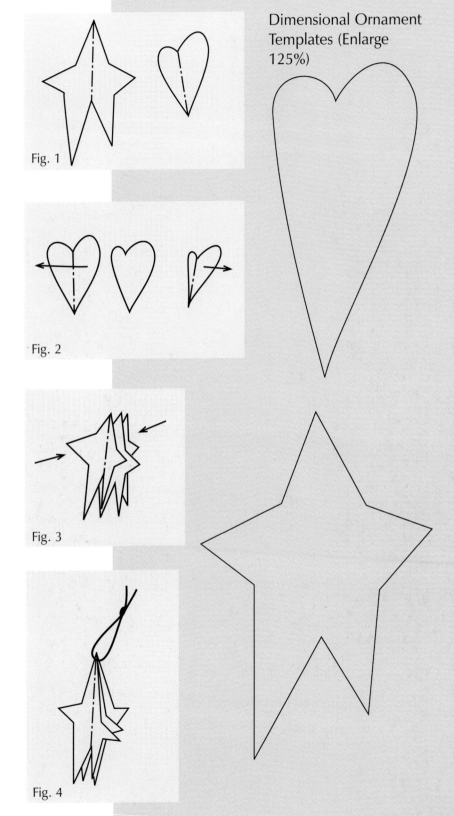

Fig. 1

Fig. 2

Fig. 3

Fig. 4

Dimensional Ornament Templates (Enlarge 125%)

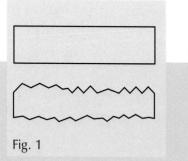

# Paper Chains

*Supplies:*
- Brown kraft paper
- Craft knife or rotary cutter
- Decorative-edged scissors: ripple
- Handmade paper
- Low-temperature glue gun and glue sticks
- Ribbon
- Ruler
- White craft glue

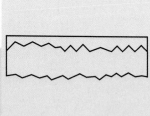

Fig. 1

Fig. 2

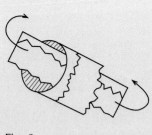

Fig. 3

*Instructions:*

1. Refer to Fig. 1. Using craft knife, cut a 1" x 5½" strip from handmade paper. Using decorative-edged scissors, cut a 1" x 5½" strip from kraft paper.

2. Refer to Fig. 2. Glue kraft paper strip onto handmade paper strip, overlapping so there is a ¼" margin along each long edge.

3. Overlap short edges and glue in place, creating a ring.

4. Repeat Steps 1–2 to make desired number of links for chain.

5. Refer to Fig. 3. Insert second strip into ring, overlap short edges, and glue in place to create linked rings. Continue making and adding links onto chain for desired length.

6. String ribbon through end rings and tie in bows for added decoration.

# Gallery of Artists

## Sarah Lugg

Sarah Lugg leads this gallery of artists who have accomplished incredible works with paper. A British artist who works in mixed media, she lives with her husband in Hampstead, London. She was raised in the beautiful countryside of the south of England, spending weekends and most holidays with her grandparents on the Isle of Wight. These formative years spent beachcombing proved to have a great influence on Sarah's work today.

After graduating in Graphic Design from Kingston University, she spent her early twenties working as a designer for Sir Terence Conran. Sarah painted and worked extensively on her own style of collages during this time. She now devotes herself purely to her collages and paintings.

Sarah's innovative mixed-media collages are enriched by her unique personal interpretations. Her work combines the sophisticated delicacy of ancient Assyrian forms with a deeply sensitive use of color and exquisite finely judged textures. Nature is also a source of unending influence on her work. Inspiration for her paintings comes from the tiny details of texture, shape, and color also found in her collages.

These transformed visions are given new dimensions as Sarah experiments with the relationship and proportions of images and backgrounds.

The unique and distinctive style of Sarah's work has led to many prestigious commissions and exhibitions. These include 30 collages for the British High Commission in Trinidad and 60 for the United Kingdom Mission to the United Nations in New York, as well as commissions from many interior design companies, art galleries, and private collectors worldwide.

Sarah has been featured several times in *Victoria* magazine and is a regular exhibitor in the United States at Artexpo and Accent on Design, where her shows are always a sellout. Following this success, her work has been published in the form of boxed sets of art cards, journals, stationery, a range of fine art prints, and a collection of exquisite wire-edged ribbons. Some of these are featured in Ballard catalog.

The overwhelming demand for her work has prompted Sarah and her husband, Robert Muller, to publish a range of signed limited edition fine art prints. Sarah is always happy to discuss private or corporate commissions.

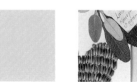

# Susan Hersey

Susan Hersey is a professional artist who, for the past 20 years, has been working with handmade paper as a medium. Her wall hangings, which consist of dyed paperpulp sprayed and collaged onto painted fiberglass or bronze screening, have been part of that evolving process. A few years ago, utilizing a pulp sprayer, she began working in a three-dimensional format.

Her sculptures are made of handmade paper pulp that is sprayed onto a wicker armature with a twig frame. They are then coated with an acrylic medium and sprayed on the inside with a flame retardant. Then a low-wattage light bulb is added for the optimal sculptural effect.

Each sculpture is one of a kind, though individual designs can be approximately recreated in concept. Susan will also work from color swatches and modify the size of a sculpture to suit a specific purpose. She has made them to smaller scale to serve as wall sconces and has custom-designed some to fit in unusual areas such as stairwells and on curved walls.

Susan's work is represented in collections worldwide.

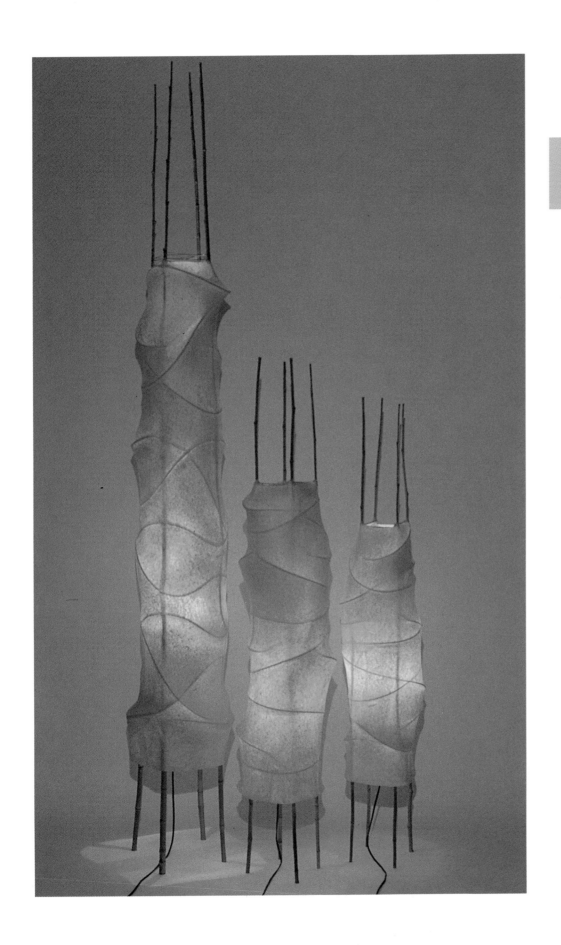

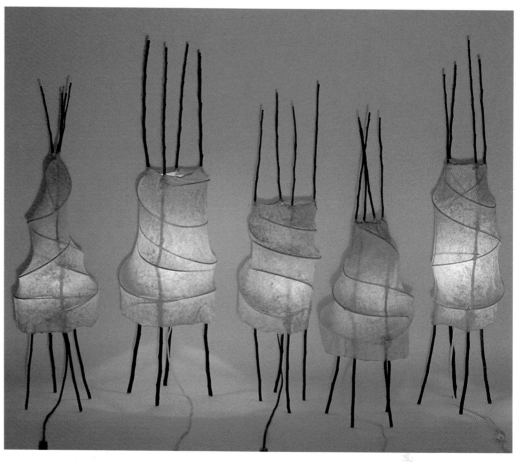

## Edgar Moises Diaz

Edgar Moises Diaz says that while growing up, he always loved to create things that were different, out of the ordinary, and fun. When there was a project to be made in elementary school, he would always try to go above and beyond. However, never in his wildest dreams did he think that he would create the artwork that he makes today.

His journey began when his wife, Kristi, wanted to purchase an expensive piece of artwork for her mother. He liked the piece, but he knew he could make something similar for much less money. She didn't believe he could do it. They did not speak about it again until her mother's birthday came around and he presented his mother-in-law with an 8" x 10" piece of artwork that he created himself. His wife was shocked at how beautiful the piece was. He says he actually surprised himself with what he was capable of doing.

Since that first creation, Edgar's work has progressed slowly but surely from making artwork for family and friends, to producing a commissioned series of 100 pieces of work.

To see someone's reaction when they look at his artwork is quite rewarding for Edgar. Most of his pieces deal with the world and social responsibility. They symbolize an ideal—all people joining together to celebrate what is right with the world. To the viewer, he hopes to put a smile on your face, hope in your heart, and an awareness for the future.

# David Dibble

David Dibble is a rising artist and illustrator who seeks to challenge the way greeting cards are generally perceived. While studying art in Venice, Italy, David was struck by the beauty and accessibility of fine Italian paper. He began experimenting with additive and reductive paper sculpture, and found that the style naturally lent itself to the idea of the greeting card. It was there that he began the greeting card company "Midnight Cards."

"I chose the name Midnight Cards perhaps to allude to the time frame in which most of my cards are done, but more specifically, to connote something romantic and mysterious. A greeting card is about the power of art, and the emotional power of words, the greeting card being a fusion of them both. Such an amazing potential for personal and emotional impact should not be underestimated."

Born and raised on a farm in Layton, Utah, David spent much of his youth exploring and sketching the surrounding countryside. His studio is located in a century-old farmhouse which overlooks the land. He continues to explore the concept of the greeting card as he pursues a degree in illustration from Brigham Young University.

Look for David's pieces on pages 40, 65, 74, 80, and 82–87.

# Vicky "Grace" Hoff

Vicky "Grace" Hoff was born in Yellowknife, Canada, in the Northwest Territories, but grew up in Laguna Beach, California. She was influenced by the seaside community of artists and family members who are also artists. She has traveled extensively throughout India, Asia, and Mexico, absorbing the different cultures into her own creativity. Her studio is now located near Durango, Colorado, in a pine forest at 7500 feet.

Grace began working with paper in 1986. Her primary passion is exploring texture and color in the field of art. For Grace, paper is a forgiving medium and lends itself to soft shapes and forms. Her artistic flair transforms the appearance of paper into the luster of metal or the texture of raku ceramic. She creates this illusion with a harmonious blend of color and design, bringing to life her unique plates, bowls, and discs.

All of Grace's "paper artifacts" pieces are carefully handcrafted and like any handmade item, each has its own inherent variations. She starts with pure cotton linter fiber and blends this with water. She then casts this mixture onto handmade forms. After drying, the cast-paper plate, bowl, or disc is hand-painted with various types of water-based paints. Gold, copper, or silver leaf is applied to some pieces, while pottery shards and found objects are cast into select others. Even though these are paper artifacts, they are reasonably durable and can be used as functional as well as aesthetic pieces.

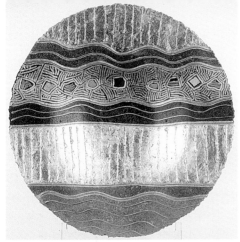

115

# Doe Cross

Doe Cross has been intrigued with the field of paper arts since childhood, when she became quite fascinated with Origami, the Japanese art of paper folding. She became so interested in paper and the art of papermaking she began taking classes, workshops, and teaching herself different techniques, all of which led to developing her own unique style. She began her current artistic career in 1989, when she started her own art studio, making an original line of handmade paper and mixed-media jewelry.

Her jewelry combines handmade paper, found objects, wood, paint, pearls, and text to construct simple, yet elegant wearable objects. Through her work, Doe strives to contrast human culture with the environment and highlight the delicate balance and fragile nature of both.

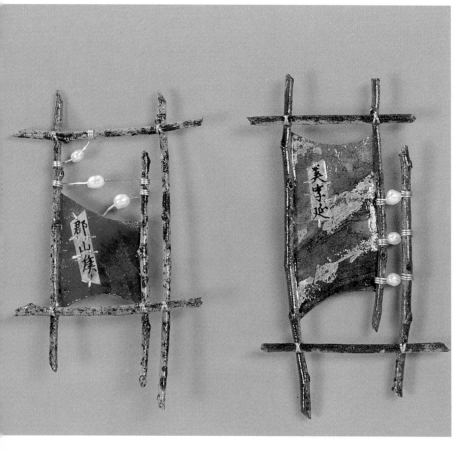

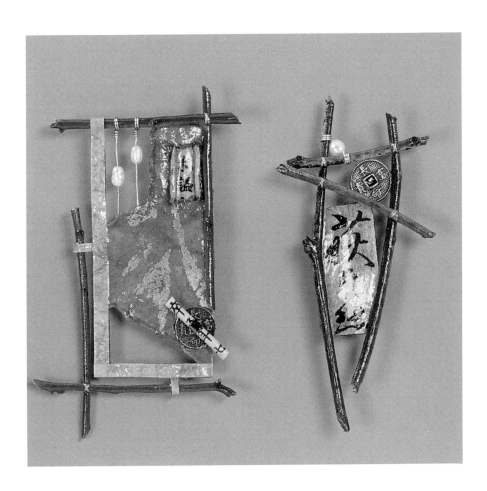

She has been told on many occasions that her jewelry pieces are fabulous miniature works of art and it has been suggested that she create them on a larger scale for the wall. In the process of taking her work to this new level, she struggles to maintain the sense of elegance, minimalism, and natural balance that she feels are intrinsic in her work.

While her new work is being received with enthusiasm, Doe feels it will continue to evolve as she explores new dimensions.

# Joan Rhine

Raised and educated in New York City, Joan Rhine worked there as a graphic designer, fine art designer, and art instructor. Her interest in handmade paper as an art medium was awakened after enrolling in an inspiring workshop given at Dieu Donne Papermill in Soho in 1979. She has been a papermaker ever since.

Her strong design background led Joan to a predilection for controlled simple forms combined with random elements. In this collection of decorative plates and bowls, Joan combines handmade paper, wire, textiles, and threads.

Joan begins each piece by making the paper from natural fibers and gradually blending in artists' pigments. In the colorful textile woven plates and bowls, she used cotton fiber. For the bowls and plates woven with metallic thread and the metal leaf lined bowls, she prepared the fiber from wild "California" grass that grows outside her studio and then combined it with abaca, a strong fiber from the orient. She creates the basic sculptural forms by 'casting' with paper pulp. To make the strips of paper for weaving, she first forms sheets of paper in a 'deckle box.'

She and her husband, artist/papermaker Jim Meilander, along with their two cats, Artemis and Lio, lived in San Francisco for 20 years. It was there that they established Submarine Paperworks at Hunter's Point Naval Shipyard. From this base overlooking the city, they created their artwork and gave workshops in hand-papermaking. They recently relocated to Gualala in Mendocino County on the north coast of California and are building a new papermaking studio on their property in the beautiful redwoods.

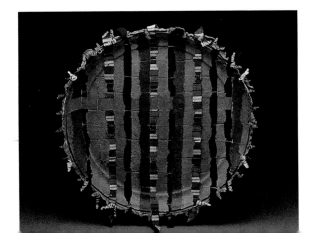

119

*all photographs by George Post*

120

# Barbara Glenn

Barbara Glenn is a fiber artist who works primarily in handmade paper. The process of papermaking—macerating the fiber, remolding their substance into new creations—coincides with her interest in the mystery of change and growth in the human spirit—regeneration and redemption. Currently she is working on a series of paper dwellings as metaphor for the human spirit in relationship to the temporary dwelling that our bodies provide—the relationship of inner space as "place" for growth and change to the outer "skin" of the dwellings. This study is an outgrowth of earlier explorations of inner/outer layers in a series of deeply layered wall pieces called Separations and Connections.

Barbara is also a teacher. She received a B.A. in Art from Bethel College in St. Paul, Minnesota, a Master's degree from the University of Minnesota where she has also taken courses toward a doctorate degree, and is an alumnus of Minneapolis College of Art and Design. Barbara has taught art at the elementary school level, the high school level, and finally at the college level. For the past sixteen years, she has been teaching college students in St. Paul, San Diego, California, and Phoenix, Arizona, where she now resides.

She has written professionally in the areas of aesthetics and art education, and has been a lecturer and demonstrator at various conferences, schools, and galleries both in the Midwest and on the West Coast. She has been guest artist at various colleges and has had her work exhibited in galleries and museums across the United States and in Europe, and included in several private collections.

Barbara was a member of California Fibers for six years while living in San Diego and has recently become a member of Arizona Designer Craftsmen.

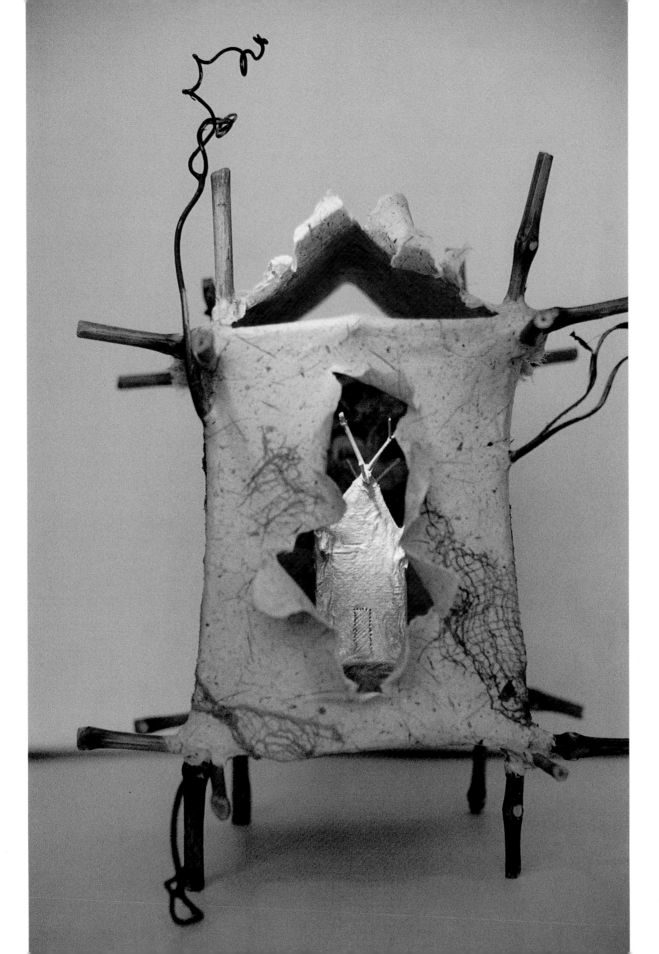

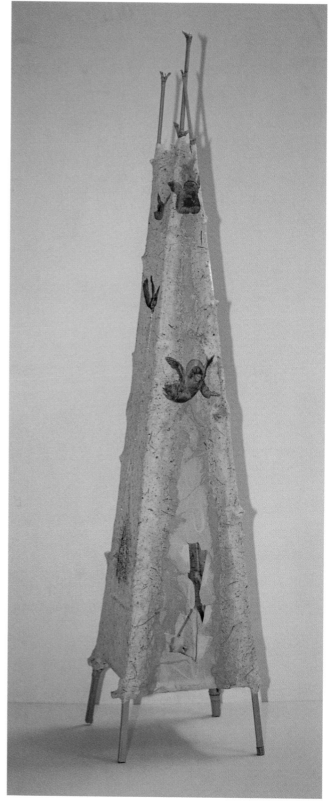

# Metric Equivalency Chart

## mm-millimetres   cm-centimetres
### inches to millimetres and centimetres

| inches | mm | cm | inches | cm | inches | cm |
|--------|----|----|--------|-----|--------|-----|
| 1/8 | 3 | 0.3 | 9 | 22.9 | 30 | 76.2 |
| 1/4 | 6 | 0.6 | 10 | 25.4 | 31 | 78.7 |
| 3/8 | 10 | 1.0 | 11 | 27.9 | 32 | 81.3 |
| 1/2 | 13 | 1.3 | 12 | 30.5 | 33 | 83.8 |
| 5/8 | 16 | 1.6 | 13 | 33.0 | 34 | 86.4 |
| 3/4 | 19 | 1.9 | 14 | 35.6 | 35 | 88.9 |
| 7/8 | 22 | 2.2 | 15 | 38.1 | 36 | 91.4 |
| 1 | 25 | 2.5 | 16 | 40.6 | 37 | 94.0 |
| 1 1/4 | 32 | 3.2 | 17 | 43.2 | 38 | 96.5 |
| 1 1/2 | 38 | 3.8 | 18 | 45.7 | 39 | 99.1 |
| 1 3/4 | 44 | 4.4 | 19 | 48.3 | 40 | 101.6 |
| 2 | 51 | 5.1 | 20 | 50.8 | 41 | 104.1 |
| 2 1/2 | 64 | 6.4 | 21 | 53.3 | 42 | 106.7 |
| 3 | 76 | 7.6 | 22 | 55.9 | 43 | 109.2 |
| 3 1/2 | 89 | 8.9 | 23 | 58.4 | 44 | 111.8 |
| 4 | 102 | 10.2 | 24 | 61.0 | 45 | 114.3 |
| 4 1/2 | 114 | 11.4 | 25 | 63.5 | 46 | 116.8 |
| 5 | 127 | 12.7 | 26 | 66.0 | 47 | 119.4 |
| 6 | 152 | 15.2 | 27 | 68.6 | 48 | 121.9 |
| 7 | 178 | 17.8 | 28 | 71.1 | 49 | 124.5 |
| 8 | 203 | 20.3 | 29 | 73.7 | 50 | 127.0 |

## yards to metres

| yards | metres | yards | metres | yards | metres | yards | metres | yards | metres |
|-------|--------|-------|--------|-------|--------|-------|--------|-------|--------|
| 1/8 | 0.11 | 2 1/8 | 1.94 | 4 1/8 | 3.77 | 6 1/8 | 5.60 | 8 1/8 | 7.43 |
| 1/4 | 0.23 | 2 1/4 | 2.06 | 4 1/4 | 3.89 | 6 1/4 | 5.72 | 8 1/4 | 7.54 |
| 3/8 | 0.34 | 2 3/8 | 2.17 | 4 3/8 | 4.00 | 6 3/8 | 5.83 | 8 3/8 | 7.66 |
| 1/2 | 0.46 | 2 1/2 | 2.29 | 4 1/2 | 4.11 | 6 1/2 | 5.94 | 8 1/2 | 7.77 |
| 5/8 | 0.57 | 2 5/8 | 2.40 | 4 5/8 | 4.23 | 6 5/8 | 6.06 | 8 5/8 | 7.89 |
| 3/4 | 0.69 | 2 3/4 | 2.51 | 4 3/4 | 4.34 | 6 3/4 | 6.17 | 8 3/4 | 8.00 |
| 7/8 | 0.80 | 2 7/8 | 2.63 | 4 7/8 | 4.46 | 6 7/8 | 6.29 | 8 7/8 | 8.12 |
| 1 | 0.91 | 3 | 2.74 | 5 | 4.57 | 7 | 6.40 | 9 | 8.23 |
| 1 1/8 | 1.03 | 3 1/8 | 2.86 | 5 1/8 | 4.69 | 7 1/8 | 6.52 | 9 1/8 | 8.34 |
| 1 1/4 | 1.14 | 3 1/4 | 2.97 | 5 1/4 | 4.80 | 7 1/4 | 6.63 | 9 1/4 | 8.46 |
| 1 3/8 | 1.26 | 3 3/8 | 3.09 | 5 3/8 | 4.91 | 7 3/8 | 6.74 | 9 3/8 | 8.57 |
| 1 1/2 | 1.37 | 3 1/2 | 3.20 | 5 1/2 | 5.03 | 7 1/2 | 6.86 | 9 1/2 | 8.69 |
| 1 5/8 | 1.49 | 3 5/8 | 3.31 | 5 5/8 | 5.14 | 7 5/8 | 6.97 | 9 5/8 | 8.80 |
| 1 3/4 | 1.60 | 3 3/4 | 3.43 | 5 3/4 | 5.26 | 7 3/4 | 7.09 | 9 3/4 | 8.92 |
| 1 7/8 | 1.71 | 3 7/8 | 3.54 | 5 7/8 | 5.37 | 7 7/8 | 7.20 | 9 7/8 | 9.03 |
| 2 | 1.83 | 4 | 3.66 | 6 | 5.49 | 8 | 7.32 | 10 | 9.14 |

# Index

## ABC

## DEF

## GHI

## JLM

## OPR

## STW